P9-CNB-229

COLIN POWELL

COLIN POWELL

A Biography

Richard Steins

GREENWOOD BIOGRAPHIES

GREENWOOD PRESS
WESTPORT, CONNECTICUT · LONDON

Library of Congress Cataloging-in-Publication Data

Steins, Richard.
    Colin Powell : a biography / Richard Steins.
        p. cm.—(Greenwood biographies, ISSN 1540–4900)
    Includes bibliographical references and index.
    ISBN 0–313–32266–X (alk. paper)
    1. Powell, Colin L. 2. Statesmen—United States—Biography. 3. Generals—United
States—Biography. 4. African American generals—Biography. 5. United States Army—
Biography. I. Title. II. Series.
E840.8.P64 S74 2003
355′.0092—dc21   2002192779

British Library Cataloguing in Publication Data is available.

Copyright © 2003 by Richard Steins

All rights reserved. No portion of this book may be
reproduced, by any process or technique, without the
express written consent of the publisher.

Library of Congress Catalog Card Number: 2002192779
ISBN: 0–313–32266–X
ISSN: 1540–4900

First published in 2003

Greenwood Press, 88 Post Road West, Westport, CT 06881
An imprint of Greenwood Publishing Group, Inc.
www.greenwood.com

Printed in the United States of America

∞™

The paper used in this book complies with the
Permanent Paper Standard issued by the National
Information Standards Organization (Z39.48–1984).

10 9 8 7 6 5 4 3 2 1

AUSTIN COMMUNITY COLLEGE
LIBRARY SERVICES

Dedicated to the memory of Caroline Steins
(1915–2001)

"We were taught that hard work and education were the keys to success.... My sister and I were taught to believe in ourselves. We might be black and considered second-class citizens, but stick with it because we were Americans. We were taught by my parents—always, always, always believe in miracles."

—Colin Powell, addressing the Republican
National Convention, 1996

CONTENTS

Photo essay follows chapter 7

SERIES FOREWORD

In response to high school and public library needs, Greenwood developed this distinguished series of full-length biographies specifically for student use. Prepared by field experts and professionals, these engaging biographies are tailored for high school students who need challenging yet accessible biographies. Ideal for secondary school assignments, the length, format, and subject areas are designed to meet educators' requirements and students' interests.

Greenwood offers an extensive selection of biographies spanning all curriculum related subject areas including social studies, the sciences, literature and the arts, history and politics, as well as popular culture, covering public figures and famous personalities from all time periods and backgrounds, both historic and contemporary, who have made an impact on American and/or world culture. Greenwood biographies were chosen based on comprehensive feedback from librarians and educators. Consideration was given to both curriculum relevance and inherent interest. The result is an intriguing mix of the well known and the unexpected, the saints and sinners from long-ago history and contemporary pop culture. Readers will find a wide array of subject choices from fascinating crime figures like Al Capone to inspiring pioneers like Margaret Mead, from the greatest minds of our time like Stephen Hawking to the most amazing success stories of our day like J. K. Rowling.

While the emphasis is on fact, not glorification, the books are meant to be fun to read. Each volume provides in-depth information about the subject's life from birth through childhood, the teen years, and adulthood. A thorough account relates family background and education, traces personal and professional influences, and explores struggles, accomplishments, and contributions. A timeline highlights the most significant life events against a historical perspective. Suggestions for further reading give the biographies added reference value.

INTRODUCTION

Colin Luther Powell, the 65th Secretary of State of the United States, has been one of the most admired Americans since he became a daily fixture on TV during the Persian Gulf War in 1991. He had been around for some time before then, serving quietly, almost anonymously, in high positions in the military and government. By the time Americans started to pay attention to him, he had risen to the highest position in the U.S. military—chairman of the Joint Chiefs of Staff—and it was as chairman that Americans took their first measure of the man.

Powell's fellow citizens have always been most impressed by his character—here was someone who was honest and straightforward, who tells it like it is. His reassuring manner, his shining intelligence, and his calmness during moments of crisis were a welcome contrast to the stream of politicians who said one thing and then did another. During the war, Powell stood before the television cameras at the Pentagon almost every day, answering questions and explaining what was happening in a war thousands of miles away. To a cynical American public used to decades of scandals and disappointments, Colin Powell was an anchor of integrity and honor. So intense was America's affection for this general that millions wanted him to run for president after he had retired from the army. It was one of the few times that Powell declined to serve—he told the American people that he did not have the burning desire to be president or to put his family through the harshness of a presidential campaign.

But who is Colin Powell? His is the story of a most unlikely hero, a man who came from a background that was not noted for its great military leaders. Colin Powell was a New York–born African American of West

Indian descent who rose to become the highest-ranking person in the U.S. military—a position he ascended to just 40 years after that very same military was desegregated. He was a man who worked for Republican presidents and was promoted by them again and again at a time when more than 90 percent of African Americans considered themselves Democrats. And he was an African American who achieved high office and became a national hero even though he was never identified with the civil rights movement.

In some respects, Colin Powell's larger-than-life image rests on these unlikely combinations. He defies conventional stereotypes. In fact, one reason he is difficult to categorize and is even somewhat mysterious is that much of his work has occurred behind the scenes. Whether in the military or in government, as National Security Adviser, Chairman of the Joint Chiefs of Staff, or Secretary of State, Powell has been an adviser to presidents. His advice is given in private, and when a presidential policy decision is announced, Powell's role in it is often the subject of speculation in the media. Ironically, he had hoped throughout most of his military career to be a commander, and although he held high command positions for brief periods, political leaders, recognizing his special abilities and extraordinary intelligence, constantly pulled him back to Washington for what one of his friends described as a career that was not conventional.

This book will examine that exceptional life and career. Colin Powell began his work life doing something he truly loved—being a soldier. His later career was devoted to the quest for peace in a ruthlessly violent world. As you will see, Powell is more than simply a soldier and a peacemaker. He is a soldier who, when sending men into battle, has always been conscious of peace; and he is a diplomat who has pursued peace with the strength and determination of a soldier. When in uniform, he tried to use military force in a way that would minimize casualties. And he cared deeply about the well-being of his men—that came first. And, as Secretary of State, he assumed responsibility for the diplomacy of his country, for the well-being of a nation in time of extreme danger.

That journey to the pinnacles of power began quietly and humbly in a family who emerged from the slave culture of Caribbean America and took a risk that their lives could be better in the United States of America.

TIMELINE

KEY DATES IN THE LIFE OF COLIN POWELL

1937   Colin Luther Powell is born on April 5 in Harlem, New York, the second child of Luther and Maud Powell, Jamaican-born immigrants.

1941   Powell family moves to the South Bronx.

1954   Begins college, enrolling at CCNY in New York.

1955   Joins CCNY's branch of the ROTC.

1957   Attends ROTC summer training at Fort Bragg, NC.

1958   Graduates from CCNY and becomes a second lieutenant in the U.S. Army.

1958   Attends Ranger school in Fort Benning, Georgia.

1958   Assigned to Third Armored Division in Gelnhausen, West Germany.

1958–1960   Stationed in West Germany.

1960   Assigned to Fort Devens, Massachusetts.

1961   Meets Alma Johnson on blind date in Massachusetts.

1962   Colin Powell and Alma Johnson married in Birmingham, Alabama.

1962   Leaves for first tour of duty in Vietnam; assigned to advise ARVN unit in A Shau Valley.

1963   Michael, first child, is born to Alma and Colin Powell.

1963   Is wounded in Vietnam; returns to United States in fall 1963.

1989   Appointed commander of FORSCOM at Fort McPherson, Georgia.

1989–1993   Named chairman of the Joint Chiefs of Staff by President Bush. Serves through the first year of the administration of President Bill Clinton.

1990–1991   Is part of the team directing U.S. forces in the Persian Gulf War.

1993   Retires from military.

1995   Autobiography, *My American Journey*, published. Powell declines to run for president.

1996   Supports Republican candidate, Bob Dole, for president.

1997   Establishes America's Promise, a volunteer organization to help America's youth.

2000   Advises George W. Bush, Republican presidential nominee, on foreign affairs.

2001   Becomes Secretary of State under President George W. Bush.

2002   Helps forge international coalition to fight terrorism; travels to Mideast to mediate Arab-Israeli conflict.

Chapter 1

STUDENT, SOLDIER, PEACEMAKER: MOMENTS IN A LIFE

FEBRUARY 1954

The campus of the College of the City of New York (CCNY) can seem frightening on first glance, especially when cold winter winds sweep down from the Hudson River, to the west, and whip around the school's imposing Gothic stone buildings. Almost European in look, CCNY is located in the northern part of Manhattan, in historic Harlem, the home to one of New York's largest African American communities. Founded in the 1890s, CCNY was unusual for a major college in that it charged no tuition. It was built to serve the children of the poor and working class who could not afford expensive private schools. Over the years, it fulfilled its mission magnificently, producing a long list of distinguished Americans in all walks of life—engineers, scientists, doctors, lawyers, even winners of the prestigious Nobel Prizes.

On a freezing morning in February 1954, a tall and thin young man approaches the campus of CCNY after a bus ride from his home in the Bronx, to the north of Manhattan. He shivers on the long walk from the bus stop on 156th Street to the entrance of the school on 141st Street and Convent Avenue. He is cold, but he is also nervous—the nervousness of a young person's first day in college. He is Colin Luther Powell, just two months shy of his seventeenth birthday, the son of proud, hardworking, Jamaican immigrants, Luther and Maud Powell. Colin had been born not far from CCNY—in Harlem, on April 5, 1937. At the age of four, his family moved to the Bronx, where he and his numerous aunts, uncles, and cousins all lived close to each other in the Hunts Point section. Colin expects to study engineering, but like many youngsters his age, he really does not know what subject he will concentrate on, and after a semester will soon switch his major to geology. But even more important, he will enroll in a U.S. Army-sponsored program on the school's campus—the ROTC (Reserve Officers Training Corps), which gives small scholarship grants to students in return for a commitment of at least three years as officers in the army following their graduation from college.

On that morning in February 1954, young Colin Powell could have no way of knowing that the decision to join the ROTC would set him on a journey that would lead him to the highest levels of the U.S. Army and the highest levels of the U.S. government. That is the future. For the time being, he has achieved a noble goal that was denied to his parents—he will attend college. Already, he has shown that he can excel and move ahead in life. But, like many teenagers, he is unsure of the direction he will take.

FEBRUARY 1963

The A Shau Valley in central Vietnam is a place of lush natural beauty. The sparsely populated region is bordered on the west by mountains, while to the east is a dense and wet rainforest. At the beginning of 1963, this part in southeast Asia was the scene of sporadic warfare. Although technically under the control of the government of South Vietnam, an ally of the United States, it was also an area in which communist North Vietnam infiltrated troops and supplies into the south. The North Vietnamese, backed by the Soviet Union and China, were determined to conquer the south and reunite the nation under communist rule. The United States, however, was determined to oppose this course of action, and by 1963 was gradually increasing the number of American forces in South Vietnam. The Americans were sent to advise the South Vietnamese military on how to resist and defeat the North Vietnamese infiltration.

In late 1962, Captain Colin Powell, now in the fifth year of his career as an army officer, was assigned to duty in Vietnam. He arrived in December and was posted as an adviser to the Second Battalion, Third Infantry Regiment, of the First Division of the Army of the Republic of Vietnam (ARVN). This 400-man unit was stationed in the A Shau Valley, where its mission was to block the infiltration by the North Vietnamese and their southern allies, the Viet Cong, and to protect the small airstrip into the valley.

Powell did not quite know what to make of his new assignment—or, for that matter, about the U.S. involvement in this part of the world. Just getting to the A Shau was itself a major undertaking, involving a harrowing ride on a U.S. Marine helicopter loaded with ARVN troops, live chickens and pigs, and other supplies. After a flight through thunderstorms, the helicopter set down on the metal airstrip and, once unloaded, took off quickly to avoid the threat of North Vietnamese small arms or artillery fire. The ARVN base was home not only to the South Vietnamese troops but also to tribespeople of the Montagnard group. The Montagnards, who were not ethnic Vietnamese, were mountain tribespeople who lived in central Vietnam.

Living in the A Shau region was like taking a shower with your clothes on. The heat and humidity were intense and constant, even in the dark shade of the rainforest, and clothing was always stained salty white from sweat. Troops were required to swallow salt tablets all the time in order to replace the loss of fluids. Despite the discomforts—and the boredom of waiting for action to begin—Powell was eager to get on with his assignment. On February 7, 1963, he and his ARVN unit embarked on what was dubbed Operation Grasshopper. Its purpose was to seek out and destroy enemy forces that were attempting to slip into South Vietnam.

The first day of the mission was uneventful. A long line of soldiers slogged through the mud fending off swarms of insects and fighting exhaustion while trying to stay alert for enemy booby traps. At night, the troops would examine their bodies for bloodsucking leeches, which would slip onto their bodies during the day as they waded through streams and across rivers.

On the sixth day of the mission, the boredom and discomfort of the march were shattered by the sound of machine-gun fire. They had been ambushed, and although Powell was not injured, several of his ARVN soldiers were killed or wounded. It was a brutal introduction to combat. Over the next weeks, ambushes became a way of life. If any of the local population were suspected of sympathizing with the North Vietnamese or Viet Cong, the ARVN forces destroyed their homes, livestock, and crops. Powell realized that this was why there were Montagnards living at the ARVN base—their villages had been torched. Although he did not question these actions at the time, Powell was disturbed by this aspect of conflict. If we were trying to help people, how could we justify destroying their villages and their livelihood and, in the process, make them dependent on the South Vietnamese army for survival?

The answers to these kinds of questions became clearer in the years after his service in Vietnam. What emerged from Powell's Vietnam experience was the evolution of ideas about when and how U.S. forces should be used in conflicts in other countries. In the early 1960s, Powell was a courageous and dedicated military man who did his duty as he was ordered. But he was also a man of conscience and revealed those qualities of mind and character that served him so well in later life: curiousness, a questioning intellect, a realistic sense of what is possible, and a healthy skepticism.

OCTOBER 2001

After a seventeen-hour flight from the United States, the huge U.S. Air Force jet, the military equivalent of the civilian Boeing-757, began its descent into Islamabad, Pakistan. This flight was unusual. Instead of gliding gradually and smoothly in toward the capital city of Pakistan, the jet bearing a high-level delegation of U.S. officials began a steep and zigzagging dive toward the airport, all of its cabin lights turned out and its passengers sitting quietly in the darkened aircraft. In his private cabin at the front of the plane was the U.S. Secretary of State, Colin Powell, now 64 years old and, since January 20, 2001, the highest-ranking cabinet official in the administration of President George W. Bush. Powell's plane was making these extraordinary maneuvers as a precaution against being shot down—not by Pakistani forces but by terrorists. Ironically, the U.S. government feared that Powell could be a target of shoulder-held, surface-to-air missiles that the Americans had given to the rebels in Afghanistan in the 1980s, when they were fighting against invaders from the neighboring Soviet Union.

Now, in 2001, the Soviet Union no longer existed, and the Afghan rebels that the U.S. government had helped twenty years earlier were sworn enemies of America. The tables had turned. It was a complicated diplomatic situation that had arisen in the wake of the attacks by terrorists on the United States on September 11, 2001, that had killed more than 3,000 people. The United States was at war against a worldwide anti-American terrorist network known as Al-Qaeda. Its major training facilities were located in Afghanistan, to the west of Pakistan, and as the U.S. prepared to attack the terrorists, it needed to make sure that the government of Pakistan was on the U.S. side and in agreement with U.S. policy.

It was not an easy task, but it was one that was part of Powell's job as Secretary of State—and one for which he was superbly prepared. The boy from the Bronx, the Vietnam hero, the soldier-turned diplomat, was now at the peak of his career and engaged in the greatest challenge he had faced to date—creating and holding together a worldwide coalition that supported the U.S. war on terrorism.

These brief moments reveal the man at key moments in his life—as a student, as a young soldier, and as a seasoned diplomat. As we examine that life in detail, we will see that Colin Powell's odyssey as a solider of peace is an American story, perhaps not a typical one, but a journey that contains all the aspects of hard work, struggle, and success that are uniquely American.

Chapter 2

FROM JAMAICA TO THE BRONX: ROOTS OF AN AMERICAN FAMILY

The island of Jamaica is a hot and fertile land in the Caribbean Sea about 90 miles south of Cuba. With some 4,400 square miles, it is slightly smaller than the state of Connecticut, and it has a population of a little over 2.5 million. Jamaica is an independent nation, but it was formerly a colony of Great Britain. Swept by warm winds and tropical rains, Jamaica has an excellent growing climate that supports a large variety of agricultural products, including sugarcane, bananas, citrus fruit, and tobacco.

Many of these crops were grown on small farms, but after the British colonized the island in 1670, they set up large plantations in order to grow commodities that could be sold in North America and in Europe. These plantations required large numbers of workers to till the fields and harvest the crops. When the English came to Jamaica, they brought with them African slaves to work the land. Africans were forced from their native lands and crammed onto small vessels for the long trip across the ocean to the Western Hemisphere. Jammed into dank holds and deprived of sanitary conditions and adequate food and water, untold numbers died on the trip across the ocean. Those who survived entered a life of slavery. Jamaica was one of many islands of the Caribbean that developed slave-based agricultural economies by the early 1700s. Other British possessions—such as the colonies on the North American mainland that were to become the United States—also imported slaves.

The British formally abolished slavery throughout their empire in the early nineteenth century. In Jamaica, slavery came to an end in the 1830s, some 30 years before it was banned in the United States after the end of the American Civil War. The former Jamaican slaves remained dreadfully poor, and the overwhelming number of them lived hard lives scraping out meager livings as small farmers. But unlike in the United States, the lives of the former slaves in Jamaica took a different path. Most of the former slaveholders lived in Britain, so there were no ex-masters looking down on and attempting to control and exploit the recently freed slaves. In addition, Jamaica was deeply influenced by English culture, especially English political institutions. Jamaica today has a British form of parliamentary government, and many English influences are still evident, including English as the country's official language. Jamaicans of all backgrounds have always had a great pride in their English politics and their political and social heritage. That tradition has included a degree of tolerance for diversity and a less self-conscious awareness of race. Many Jamaicans are a mix of Caucasian, Indian, and African stock, to name just three ethnic groups found on the island.

Sixty miles west of the capital city of Kingston, and just a few miles north of the Caribbean coast, lies the small town of Top Hill. The people of Top Hill are poor and hard working. They work the red soil and maintain small, neat homes, many of which still have no electricity, plumbing, or running water. Floors are often just made of dirt, and people live close to the land; a kitchen might often be shared with chickens as they scurry in and out of the house.

Into such a typical and humble home in 1898 was born Luther Powell, the man who would become the father of Colin Powell. Luther, the second of nine children, grew up in a four-room house with a tin roof that was nestled in the gentle fields and shaded by a large guongo tree. In front of the green and orange house was a small graveyard containing the remains of Powell ancestors.

By the time he was in his early twenties, Luther decided on a course of action that many young men in his generation chose—he wanted to migrate to the United States in search of a better life. Although he loved Jamaica, he was drawn to the United States in the hope of finding a good job and a place that would offer him and any children he might have greater opportunities than those found in a small village in Jamaica.

Luther's future wife, Maud Ariel McKoy of Westmoreland, in western Jamaica, shared the same dream, and she too made the journey to the United States around the same time that Luther did. Unlike Luther, Maud had completed high school and worked as a stenographer before moving to America. Many other members of the Powell and McKoy families migrated to the United States in the early part of the twentieth century, where they formed the core of the large, extended family into which Colin Powell would be born and raised.

Moving to another country is a momentous decision, especially for young people who had grown up in small towns and whose whole world had never extended beyond their immediate surrounding areas. Today, Jamaica is just four or five hours from New York by air and is a popular tourist destination for vacationers from all over the world. But in the 1920s, when young Luther and Maud decided to move to the United States, the only way to go was by ship. And not a large cruise ship either, but a small banana boat. After docking in Philadelphia, Luther headed for New York City and for their new life in America.

Luther Powell was not a large man. Unlike his famous son, who is more than six feet tall, Luther's height was only five feet, two inches. The Powells and the McCoys, like many Jamaican families, had a rich ethnic heritage that included African, English, Irish, Scottish, and (some in the family believed) Arawak Indian stock. Nevertheless, Luther and Maud Powell would have been perceived as black in the eyes of 1920s America, and it was as blacks that their lives were organized and lived out.

As he began his new life in the United States, Luther Powell first worked as a gardener and as a building superintendent. He eventually found a job at a company in Manhattan that manufactured women's clothing—a job at which he remained for the remainder of his working life. Luther started in the shipping department as a clerk and over the years was promoted, rising to the position of foreman of the department. Colin Powell remembers him as a proud and self-assured man who, despite his short stature, stood tall. He was always well dressed, and he carried himself as a proud man who knew what he valued in life.

Colin's mother also worked. A small and stout woman who was an inch shorter than her husband, Maud worked in the garment industry and was a member of the International Ladies Garment Workers Union (ILGWU). Family legend has it that Luther and Maud met at Maud's mother's apartment in Harlem, although the exact nature of their first meeting is not certain. Colin's maternal grandmother, Alice McKoy, known as "Gram," took care of Colin when his parents were at work and was also a major force in the family, where she tended to the needs of her children and their children and rented rooms in her apartment to new immigrants who arrived in New York from Jamaica.

The Powell's first child, a daughter named Marilyn, was born in 1931, a full decade after the hardworking couple had arrived in this country. When Colin was born, on April 5, 1937, the family was living on Morningside Avenue in the Harlem area of Manhattan. When Colin was four, his family moved to the Hunts Point section of the Bronx. By 1943, his family was living in a four-bedroom apartment on the third floor of 952 Kelly Street.

It was from this home that Colin would go to school and church and grow into adulthood. Numerous aunts and uncles from both the Powell and McKoy branches of the family ultimately found apartments on Kelly Street. The sense of the extended family was strong and real.

Life in America during the 1930s was deeply influenced by the catastrophe of the economic Depression that began with the stock market crash of 1929. More than 25 percent of the workforce was unemployed and the percentages were higher among people of color. At that time, there was no such thing as Social Security or Medicaid. The poor and the unemployed had to fend for themselves, and if things went bad, people had only their families and charity to help them get through the hard times. It was not an unusual sight in New York City, in the 1930s, to see people lining up at soup kitchens for a simple, but free meal, or to see the unemployed begging in the streets for a nickel or penny. People were homeless, and New York's Central Park had a population who lived in tents and caves.

The Powells were fortunate during this terrible time. Both Luther and Maud held jobs and were able to provide for their children and even help other members of the family who came up from Jamaica. The Hunts Point neighborhood during the 1930s and 1940s was a true mix of many ethnic backgrounds and religions. Colin's family attended the nearby St. Margaret's Episcopal Church, where Luther was a warden, Maud headed the church's altar guild, Marilyn played the piano, and Colin served as an altar boy. The neighborhood also had synagogues and Protestant churches, and in addition to West Indians, there were also Jews, Irish, Germans, Poles, Italians, and blacks. As Colin remembered it: "The South Bronx was an exciting place when I was growing up, and I have never longed for those elms and picket fences."[1] And, of course, the streets of Hunts Point did not have elm trees and picket fences. Instead, it had tenement apartment houses, a true urban landscape crowded with families from all parts of the globe, but all looking basically for the same things—especially a better life and greater opportunity for their children and future generations.

What kind of a boy was Colin Powell? He remembers himself as being directionless. As he said in his autobiography published in 1995, "I was not fired by anything."[2] He enjoyed hanging out with friends and going to the movies on Saturdays. And he got into trouble on occasion. One summer, when attending a church camp near Peekskill, New York, Colin and some friends sneaked out of camp and bought beer. They attempted to hide it, but their stash was soon discovered, and the camp officials wanted to know who was responsible for the transgression. Colin confessed and was sent home, but the fact that he had been honest and confessed almost immediately lessened the disappointment felt by his parents.

The adult Colin Powell was able to look back and see himself as a fairly unmotivated child, but he grew up in the care of loving and (in the best sense of the word) strict parents who made sure he remained on the right path. Colin may have liked to hang out with friends, but he also went to church with his family every Sunday, and in his teen years, he had a part-time job at Sickser's, a Jewish-owned neighborhood store that sold baby furnishings and toys.

Looking back as an adult, Colin Powell did not remember having feelings as a child or teenager of being a member of a minority. From his vantage point, everyone in his neighborhood was a member of a minority group—there were so many people of different backgrounds that no one dominated the neighborhood. But the primary reason for this early lack of racial identity (to use his words)[3] was a similar lack of racial self-consciousness on the part of his parents and immediate family. The Powells and McKoys believed that anyone—regardless of skin color—could have success in life if he worked hard and applied himself. Education was sacred, and Colin's older sister was the first in the family to go off to college. In 1950, Colin entered Morris High School. His best friend was also of West Indian descent, but other friends included kids who were from Jewish, Irish, black, and other ethnic backgrounds. Powell reflected in later life that although racial terms were often thrown around—teenagers have a unique capacity to tease and at times be cruel—there was never an underlying sense of one person being superior to another. Colin would experience racism, as does every person of color in the United States—but only after leaving Kelly Street and venturing out into the wider world.

Colin Powell finished high school in early 1954, just a couple of months shy of his seventeenth birthday. Sixteen is a young age to go off to college, even if the college is in a nearby borough and one is staying at home and not living in a dormitory. When he began college, Colin expected to study engineering. After exposure to the many subjects a college freshman is introduced to, Colin came to the conclusion that engineering was not the best choice for a major. Instead, he chose geology. When his decision was announced to his parents, it precipitated a family crisis. Aunts and uncles were consulted, and questions were raised. "Was this a good subject to study?" "What kind of job would Colin be able to get as a graduate with a degree in geology?" "Should he be encouraged to choose another major?"

As it turned out, the family concerns were misdirected. The big choice in Colin Powell's young life was not to be between engineering and geology. Shortly after starting college, Colin became interested in the Reserve Officers Training Corp (ROTC). Once on this army-bound path, he would not look back. In later years, Powell reflected on why he had joined the ROTC, especially coming from a family where there was no tradition whatsoever of service in the military. He recalled having seen a couple of ROTC members walking across the campus in their attractive uniforms, but other than that, Powell had no strong recollection about why, as a seventeen-year-old in his first year in college, he decided to join the military.

In high school, Powell had been an average student, graduating with a 78 percent average. In college, his grade averages were around C. In other words, as a student, he did not do poorly, nor did he excel. But when ROTC entered his life, he found something that truly motivated him. As he later wrote, "All I ever looked forward to was ROTC."[4] The year 1954 was only one year after the end of the Korean War and a mere nine years since America's greatest conflict, World War II, had ended. The draft was still in place, which meant that young American men had to decide what to do regarding their obligations to the military: Should one enlist and deal with it that way, or would it be better to await the notice from the draft board?

ROTC offered college-age men one alternative, and one that allowed an opportunity to plan for future military service while finishing one's college education. But it also offered the possibility for a long-range career in the military. What Powell discovered as he participated in the program was his total enjoyment of the comradeship and the sense of belonging. In many ways, his close-knit family, with his parents' strong values, belief in hard work, and love of country had been an excellent preparation for an organization where discipline, loyalty, and patriotism mattered.

Members of ROTC took on a heavy workload in addition to their college studies. Added to their normal number of classes, study time, reading, and exams were the requirements of the ROTC program. That included lots of drill work—marching, learning about weapons and army life, and army-related academic studies. Colin soon discovered that he was attracted to an elite organization within the ROTC called the Pershing Rifles (PRs). In this fraternity, Colin made many life-long friendships. The PRs studied and drilled together, spent their free time together, and partied together.

When not studying or drilling with his ROTC buddies, Colin Powell was a normal New York teenager of the 1950s. During the summer he held a job at a soda bottling plant to earn extra money, starting as a janitor and working his way up to working the bottling machines. In his third year at college, he enrolled in advanced ROTC. Most Saturdays during the school year were spent at ROTC, where the cadets drilled, marched, and learned army traditions.

Colin's parents were somewhat mystified by their son's interest in the military, but they were proud of him. They assumed he would do his required service after graduating from college and then would return to civilian life and get a real job. Their lives, as well, were changing. With the proceeds from a winning numbers game, Luther Powell put a down payment on a house in the Hollis section of New York City's borough of Queens. The Powells, like generations of immigrants before them, were realizing, step-by-step, the American dream. The Hunts Point section of the Bronx was in decline. It had not been a perfect neighborhood, even when the Powells first moved there in the 1940s. It had its share of crime, and as Colin observed, families always kept their doors locked. But the neighborhood's diversity had also been its strength. Families learned that people of different religious and ethnic backgrounds were also human, and tolerance and friendships could be built across color line. But now it was time for the Powells to move on. From his new home, Colin began commuting to Manhattan from Hollis, Queens.

In the summer of 1957, the ROTC required Colin to do summer training at Fort Bragg, North Carolina. The summer at Fort Bragg was spent in rifle practice and the introduction to other military subjects such as artillery and camouflage. Powell remembered how anxious his father was at the prospect of his son going into the Deep South for the first time, where he faced the reality of segregation and anti-black prejudice. Although the U.S. military had been desegregated on the orders of President Harry Truman in the late 1940s, American society remained segregated, especially in the South. And there were always the attitudes that were not officially against the law, but which could be painful for a young black man to have to confront for the first time—the snubs, the glances, the restrictions against blacks in public places such as restrooms and restaurants. On his way back to New York City, driving with two other white colleagues from ROTC, Colin got a strong taste of racism. Gas station restrooms were segregated: Men, women, and colored, which often meant that black men and women were forced to use the same restroom.

Back in New York, Colin entered his final year in college, receiving average grades in his academic studies but all A's in ROTC subjects. Soon after the school year began, he was informed by the ROTC unit's commanding officer that he was to be promoted to cadet colonel. That meant that he was to be the student leader of the entire thousand-man ROTC unit at CCNY. In addition, he was also elected company commander of the Pershing Rifles. Even before formally entering the U.S. Army, Colin Powell was in a command position.

On June 9, 1958, Colin Powell became a second lieutenant in the U.S. Army in a ceremony at Aronowitz Auditorium at City College. With his parents and other family members in attendance, he accepted the commission that made him a member of the American military for the next three years. That evening, Colin and his buddies partied late at the nearby Emerald Bar, but Maud sent a cousin to get Colin to make sure that he came home and got enough sleep for the following day—June 10, his graduation from college.

The next stop was Fort Benning, Georgia.

NOTES

1. Colin Powell, with Joseph E. Persico, *My American Journey* (New York: Random House, 1995), p. 11.

2. Ibid., p. 16.

3. Ibid., p. 19.

4. Ibid., p. 26.

Chapter 3

"THE CARE OF OUR MEN": AN ARMY EDUCATION

After three years in the ROTC, Colin Powell was ready to begin his career in the military; and no place could have been a more abrupt transition than the army infantry school at Fort Benning, Georgia. A summer of infantry training in the steamy climate of northwestern Georgia was guaranteed to produce at least two results: a well-trained soldier and a considerably thinner soldier.

The infantry is the heart and soul of the army. Infantry soldiers are the foot soldiers, the ones who fight the battles on the ground. Infantrymen carry rifles; they march into battle supported by tanks, air cover, and artillery. They are the troops who crash through the enemy lines, march into enemy territory, and, in the end, defeat the enemy's forces.

Young army officers as well as the average draftee or enlisted grunt all take infantry training that is as grueling as any in the military services. In the summer of 1958, Colin Powell moved to the next level in the army. The ROTC courses, located in buildings nestled in the urban sprawl of CCNY, were left behind. The safe camaraderie of the college military program gave way to the real-world grit of an army base and a no-nonsense training program. Now came the shock of training designed not only to teach specific skills, but also to toughen the officers and make them fit to lead other men and to test the levels of their endurance and character.

The first stage of the initiation was an intensive basic infantry course. Then followed a period of even more difficult training to become an elite Army Ranger. The Ranger training included scaling cliffs, crossing deep rivers by crawling on a thin rope, and rappelling quickly down steep mountainsides. The trainees spend days in the outdoors, where they camp out at night and by day slog through swamps. Powell was interested in being a paratrooper as well—an airborne Ranger. To do so, he would need to conquer any fear he had about jumping out of an airplane. In the second week of training, the soldier is required to jump off a 250-foot-high tower. In the third week, however, the future paratrooper is taken up in an Army C-123 transport and told to jump. Powell, like any other trainee, felt the raw fear of standing in the open doorway of a moving plane thousands of feet in the air. But he jumped. In fact, in the first two days of his third week of airborne training, he made five jumps. The ability to overcome his fears was exhilarating. Not only was he able to leap from an airplane, but he had proven his abilities to endure one of the most strenuous physical courses in the U.S. military and come out on top.

Powell's second journey to the Deep South also reinforced the experiences and impressions he had during his first brief visit south of the Mason-Dixon Line when he was a ROTC student at Fort Bragg. The American Civil Rights movement was on the brink of achieving its great legislative victories of the 1960s, victories that led to the abolition of segregation in public accommodations and to the guarantee of voting rights to African Americans in the South. But in the late 1950s, these changes were still a few years away. In many southern states, Colin Powell could still not eat at lunch counters frequented by whites, nor could he use a men's rest room in a public place. For a young man whose family had not been racially conscious and who had grown up in one of New York's most diverse neighborhoods, these insults were a shock and a deep humiliation.

When he was an older man, Powell reflected on his attitude to the racial injustice he encountered when he was a young soldier in the South. He was determined to ignore the slights and the insults, no matter how painful. It was not that he was afraid or that he was not filled with rage at being treated like a second-class citizen. He chose, instead, not to confront his tormentors but to focus instead on achieving his goals and being the best soldier he could. Like any human being, Powell had a temper; but he was steadfast in his refusal to allow his temper and anger to derail his chances in the army. Instead of giving way to the momentary pleasure of a direct confrontation with somebody—which most likely would have resulted in his being arrested—he decided to set an example of excellence and show any detractors that a black man could be as good as, if not better than, any white man in uniform.

After training at Fort Benning, Powell received his first assignment. He would be sent to the Third Armored Division in Gelnhausen, West Germany. In the late 1950s, the United States was entangled in a serious and at times frightening rivalry with the Soviet Union, a conflict that was called the Cold War. One of the focal points of the Cold War was Germany, which on its defeat at the end of World War II in French zones of occupation, united as the Federal Republic of Germany (West Germany), which was allied with the United States. That same year, the Soviet zone of occupation became the German Democratic Republic, which remained allied with the Soviet Union. Germany was thus divided down the middle, and on its territory, both East and West, were stationed huge armies and some nuclear weapons. An assignment to Germany in the late 1950s was like going to the front line during wartime. The U.S. Army faced eastward, toward the line dividing West and East Germany. On the other side, facing westward, were the Soviet armies. The only thing missing was the shooting.

Gelnhausen was some twenty-five miles east of the city of Frankfurt and only forty miles west of the border of East Germany. If the Russians ever decided to invade West Germany, their tanks would roll westward right over Gelnhausen. The mission of Powell's unit, therefore, was quite simple: stop any Soviet invasion of West Germany. Powell's immediate command in the Third Armored Division was Company B, Second Armored Rifle Battalion, of the Forty-eighth Infantry Regiment. As a platoon leader, Powell commanded a unit that was as diverse as his old neighborhood in the Bronx.

But what do armies do when there is no shooting war, other than trying to prevent their men from getting into trouble while on leave? In Germany, they drilled and practiced, and practiced and drilled. And they had a vitally important responsibility. The Third Armored Division had a powerful nuclear weapon in its arsenal—a 280-millimeter atomic cannon, which was so enormous that it had to be hauled around on two tractor-trailers. In order to prevent the Soviets from pinpointing the location of these weapons, they were continuously hauled around the forests of West Germany from one spot to another, changing position in order to keep the Russians guessing their whereabouts. Powell's company was called on to guard this mammoth artillery piece, and it was a responsibility that Powell undertook with the utmost seriousness.

While in Germany, Powell was also frequently tapped for special assignments. Once he was ordered to act as the prosecutor at the court-martial of an enlisted man whose reckless driving had resulted in the death of three German civilians. On another occasion, he was given a two-month temporary assignment as the head of a special honor guard. At the time, Powell was worried that frequent special assignments would sidetrack his career by taking him away from command positions. In fact, they were recognition that he was intelligent and had special skills with people, skills that would be more and more valued as his career progressed.

Powell prided himself on his ability to get along with all kinds of people, even the most difficult, but he faced a tough taskmaster in the form of Captain William C. Louisell Jr., a career officer who was one of his company commanders during his tour in Germany. Louisell was that rare individual in Colin Powell's career—a man who gave him a somewhat negative written evaluation, criticizing him for showing an explosive temper when dealing with a fellow officer. In typical fashion, Powell took the criticism in stride and worked hard to monitor his temper, as he had done when facing the insults of racial prejudice. Although his temper showed itself only on rare occasions, he needed to be aware of it. Like the young officer in the segregated South, Powell understood that his emotions could be his friend or his enemy. They were his to use.

And fits of temper were certainly understandable in the army in Germany. The army at that point contained many draftees who had been pulled from their jobs or from school for a two-year stint. There were also the enlisted men, those who had voluntarily joined the army. Many of them were less educated than the draftees, and a natural tension arose rooted in the irony that those who didn't want to be in the military were often brighter and more qualified than those who wanted to be there. This, along with the inevitable boredom that comes to a fighting force during times of peace, often led to discipline problems and fights. Some of the soldiers had the misfortune to get in trouble with German civilians and civil authorities. Powell, as a low-ranking officer, was forced to deal with these and other problems as they arose in his platoon. In his later years, he would write about the understandings he had acquired during his early career in Germany. He wrote, "Gelnhausen was my introduction into what the army is really about—soldiers. Here in the Forty-eighth Infantry, life revolved around the care of our men."[1] It was a crucial lesson, and one that he never forgot and that motivated him in every position he held as he advanced to the top of the military and diplomatic world.

At the end of 1960, Colin Powell completed his two-year tour of duty in Germany. It was time to return home, to renew contacts with his family, and to move on to another assignment. That assignment was Fort Devens, Massachusetts, and the First Battle Group, Fourth Infantry, Second Infantry Brigade. This unit was commanded by Brigadier General Joseph Stilwell Jr., the son of the late General Joseph Stilwell who had fought the Japanese in China during World War II and had earned the famous nickname "Vinegar Joe." Powell eventually became the executive officer and then commander of Company A and later was shifted to the position of adjutant of a new unit, the First Battalion of the Second Infantry. An adjutant handles many personnel issues such as promotions, leaves, assignments, and the like. It was not the kind of job that Powell enjoyed, although he did it without complaint, preferring instead to have a command position of a combat unit.

In the summer of 1961, Powell's three-year commitment to the army was over, and he was free to return to civilian life. His parents expected that he would, so it came as a surprise to them when he announced that he would not resign but would continue in the army. He was a soldier through and through. He had no intention of leaving the army he loved.

But it was time in life for another love. Colin had had girlfriends when he was a teenager and a young man, but in his early years in the army, there was no time to think of marriage and family. While at Fort Devens, a friend named Michael Heningburg, who was also from Queens, asked Powell if he would like to go on a double date. Heningburg's girlfriend lived in Boston, and she had a roommate. Would Powell consider a blind date with the girl? Colin told his friend that he was not interested in meeting a new girlfriend, but Heningburg kept pressing, and in the end, Powell agreed. They went to Boston. It was November 1961.

In Boston, Heningburg's girlfriend, Jackie Fields, was having an equally difficult time convincing her roommate to go on a blind date with her boyfriend's pal from Fort Devens. After some cajoling, she reluctantly agreed. That was how Colin Powell met his wife, Alma Johnson. After their first meeting, they found they were both interested in each other enough to follow up with another date.

Alma was a beautiful, shy, and soft-spoken woman from Birmingham, Alabama. Her father was the principal of one of the city's two black high schools, and her uncle was the principal of the other. Alma's mother was deeply involved in the black Girl Scouts and was a leader in the Congregational Church. Alma herself was a graduate of Fisk University in Tennessee and was in Boston doing graduate work in audiology at Emerson College and working at an organization dedicated to helping the hard of hearing.

A month or so after they met, Colin decided it would be nice if Alma met his family in New York. They arranged to meet for a New Year's Eve party with the family. Alma's relatives were, on the surface, quite different from Colin's. Her parents were reserved and socially conservative. Alma had been brought up to observe all the proper manners expected of a young lady in the 1950s. Colin's family, by contrast, was large, and, in his words, were "nosy, noisy, fun-loving West Indians."[2] Their idea of a party meant having untold quantities of food to eat, good rum to drink, and lots of calypso music to dance to.

Differences in their families, however, were less important than the issues facing any young couple in an emerging relationship. The first was the question of Colin's profession. If he and Alma were to marry, what would her life be like as an army wife? Would she want to have such a life, with the prospect of moving from base to base and country to country, and with periods where her husband could be away from home for months, even years? For Colin, the issue seemed more essential. Did he want to marry at all? Was he ready now—or ever—to settle down, especially since the life of a professional soldier would likely be difficult for anyone raising a family?

Alma had a chance to observe army life up close on her visits from Boston to Fort Devens; and from the beginning, she liked Colin's friends and got along well with them and their wives. But the event that brought their relationship into focus was Colin's next assignment. In August 1962, he received orders to go to South Vietnam. He would be gone for a year. For Colin, this new assignment was an important career opportunity. President John F. Kennedy had decided that the United States would send Americans to Vietnam to advise the South Vietnamese armed forces in their struggle against the Viet Cong—a Communist guerrilla force backed by the Communist government of North Vietnam. American military advisers would witness combat up close and would be defending freedom on another front line—just as they did in West Germany, Colin's first posting.

The conflict in Vietnam would become one of the most bitterly divisive events in U.S. history. Before it ended in 1975, the United States would end up committing hundreds of thousands of troops, engage in direct combat, and suffer more than 58,000 soldiers killed. But that was all in the future. In 1962, Vietnam was just an advisory mission.

After a year, he would return and resume his relationship with Alma. He told her he hoped she would write, but to his shock and surprise, she said she would NOT write to him. She had no intention of waiting a year for him to return. Colin was shocked. What did he really want? After mulling over her response, Colin proposed to Alma the next day and she accepted. They planned to get married in two weeks, on August 25, 1962, in Birmingham, Alabama. Before the wedding took place, a momentary flap occurred when Luther announced he would not attend, not because he didn't like Alma (he adored her), but because the wedding was being held in the Deep South, and he would not go anywhere where his skin color would result in him being disrespected. After the rest of the family—including Powell's sister Marilyn and her white husband Norman—announced that they were attending, Luther relented.

Colin now had to face the nerve-racking moment of meeting his soon-to-be father-in-law. Alma's dad was formidable—intelligent, serious, somber-faced, and, as it turned out, not terribly fond of West Indians. (He considered them lower-class blacks.) But he liked and respected Colin and the wedding, held on a sweltering afternoon in the Congregational Church, went off without a hitch. After a wedding reception, the newlyweds spent the night in Birmingham before flying back to Fort Devens.

Fort Devens was to be a brief interlude in the newlyweds' life. By September, Colin and Alma headed off to Fort Bragg, North Carolina, where he began training as a military assistance adviser at the Unconventional Warfare Center. In the early 1960s, the U.S. government put a great deal of hope into the concept of military advisers as a means of fighting communism in foreign countries. Instead of having to commit thousands of American troops to direct combat in foreign lands, the government hoped that sending military advisers would be a more efficient way of resisting communist aggression.

In retrospect, especially in light of what eventually occurred in Vietnam, the idea seems naïve and overly simplistic. But in 1962, Colin Powell, like many fellow officers, was idealistic and eager to be a part of the defense of his country and its values. He had guarded the atomic cannons in Germany and been at the ready for a Soviet invasion of Western Europe. In Vietnam, he would be defending the world against communism at the opposite end of the globe.

Alma's concerns, however, were far more practical. At Fort Bragg, the couple lived in a spare bedroom in the home of the Schwar family. Joe Schwar was an army buddy of Colin's from his days in Germany, and he and his wife generously offered a room to Colin and Alma, who were having trouble finding decent housing in the segregated environs of Fort Bragg. By the time December rolled around, it was time for Colin to start packing. And, by now, Alma was also expecting their first child. After Colin left for Vietnam, Alma would return to Birmingham and stay with her family until he came back from Vietnam.

Colin Powell traveled from North Carolina to Travis Air Force Base in California, the staging area for Vietnam-bound troops. Travis is near Sacramento, California, and within a few minutes of takeoff, westward bound aircraft are over the Pacific. The long flight is interrupted with brief stops in Hawaii, and, sometimes, the Philippines, Okinawa, or Guam. A trans-Pacific flight is an awesome reminder of how large that ocean is, and how far away the destination country is from the United States. So far, and yet so near. Vietnam—a small country that most Americans had probably not heard of in 1962—would figure large in U.S. history and would contribute to the making of the spectacular career of Colin Powell. It would also be yet another time when Colin Powell would learn that the care of our men is one of the major responsibilities he faced as a military man.

NOTES

1. Powell, *My American Journey*, p. 49.
2. Ibid., p. 64.

Chapter 4

VIETNAM: THE POLITICS OF LAST RESORT

Saigon, the capital city of South Vietnam, was an Asian city with a French accent. The French, who were Vietnam's colonial masters from the nineteenth century until the Vietnamese forced them out in 1954, left a permanent mark on the city on the Mekong River. Many Vietnamese spoke French, and French-style architecture was seen all over the city. French colonial administrators built lovely villas on the tree-lined side streets of Saigon. In the central part of the city, French restaurants and hotels reminded visitors of the city's colonial past.

In downtown Saigon was one such hotel: the Rex. By 1962, it had been converted into an officers' billet for incoming U.S. advisers. After landing in Saigon, Colin Powell went to the Rex, where he remained for a short time before heading off to his first assignment in the A Shau Valley (see chapter 1). Saigon's streets reverberated with the ever-present putt-putt sound of motor scooters and the tooting of taxi horns and mini busses. For those not well off enough to afford motorized transportation, there were thousands of pedicabs—three-wheeled bicycle taxis that held two people and were pedaled by a driver. Young women strolled the streets dressed in the traditional Vietnamese *ao dai,* a flowing, ankle-length dress with a front and rear panel and decorated in bright colors and elegant patterns.

Saigon was exciting and exotic—but for most U.S. soldiers, it was only a momentary stopover on the way to the countryside and the war. Powell's early experiences in the A Shau Valley were typical of those faced by other advisers: the heat, the danger, the intermittent boredom, the hunger for news from home, and the longing to see loved ones again. The A Shau Valley, with all its discomfort and dangers, was a swift immersion into the Vietnam experience.

In March 1963, Powell's unit was given a new assignment; they were ordered to build a new base camp at Le Buong, which was located in the southeastern part of the A Shau Valley. There, he continued to work with Captain Vo Cong Hieu, the commander of the Vietnamese army unit Powell had been advising. It was an excellent introduction to working with someone from a completely different cultural background. Hieu knew a few words of English, and he was a family man. The prospective father and the experienced father became friends despite a cultural divide and a language barrier. In addition, Powell found Hieu to be an intelligent, caring, and skillful commander. Vietnamese troops were not the easiest to work with or to train. Despite care and attention, they were often undisciplined; the desertion rate was high, and morale was often low. It would be a problem the United States would face throughout its time in Vietnam. But Powell and Hieu were a good team; they worked side by side in the backbreaking task of carving out a base camp from the dense forest, all the time facing the possibility of attack from the enemy lurking in the surrounding jungle.

Shortly after the camp had been established, Hieu was transferred, and his replacement, a Captain Kheim, lacked the skills that Powell had found so impressive in Hieu. Kheim was an impatient man prone to temper tantrums. He often made poor decisions, such as firing in the night at Viet Cong mortars from a high hill—thus announcing to the Viet Cong where his forces were. Powell urged him not to fire back, since it was clear from the position of Viet Cong incoming shells that they did not know where the South Vietnamese unit was located. By firing back in the dark, they would give themselves away. Kheim disagreed and ordered the counterfire. Within a few minutes, Viet Cong mortars were raining down on Powell and his unit. He was unhurt, but it was a close call.

As had been the case in Germany, Powell was frequently called away from his unit for special assignments. In the spring of 1963, he was summoned to regimental headquarters at Quang Tri to be briefed on the latest thinking about the war from Washington. On this visit, Powell met Major George B. Price, a black officer who advised another Vietnamese unit and who was the brother of the world famous opera singer, Leontyne Price. George Price became a good friend and an important mentor in Powell's career. A couple of months later, Powell was ordered to travel to the old imperial city of Hue, where he was informed that he had been selected to attend the Infantry Officers Advanced Course at Fort Benning after his return from Vietnam. The selection to this course was an honor that promised to open a door for a promotion to the highest ranks in the army. When he heard the news, Powell was incredulous. He had only re-cently graduated from the basic infantry course, yet here he was being of-fered a fast track to higher rank in the service.

But first, he had to finish his tour of Vietnam in one piece; and he was still on edge about the birth of his first child. He and Alma had an agree-ment about how he was to be told. After the baby was born, she would write a letter and would print on the envelope in large letters "BABY LETTER." By prior agreement, his buddies at regimental headquarters in Quang Tri would keep an eye out for this letter, and when it arrived, Pow-ell gave them permission to open it and to radio the contents to him at Le Boung. As fate would have it, the letter went astray, and Powell found out that he was a father for the first time by reading about it in another letter from his mother. Michael Kevin Powell was born on March 23, 1963, in Birmingham, Alabama. Powell was relieved that everything had gone as well as it did and that mother and child were healthy and happy. Now, more than ever, it was important for him to stay healthy himself and to re-turn to the United States.

But he had a close call. In July 1963, Powell's unit was ordered to leave the Le Buong camp and to go to a Special Forces camp for a brief rest. With Powell at its head, the unit began its march through the jungle. As they trudged along a creek bed, Powell's right leg suddenly dropped into a shallow hole. He felt a sharp pain in his foot and knew immediately what had happened. He had fallen victim to one of the Viet Cong's simplest and most lethal weapons—shallow holes in the jungle floor that were concealed with brush and other vegetation. In the hole was a "punji stick." This piece of wood was whittled as sharp as a razor, and its tip was smeared with buffalo dung. When the unsuspecting soldier stepped into the trap, the punji stick pierced the sole of his boot and stabbed him in the foot. The wound may not have seemed serious in the beginning, but since the sticks were contaminated with dung, the victim soon came down with a severe and potentially life-threatening infection and fever. At the very least, a punji stick wound immobilized the victim and made him useless in combat.

Powell was angry that he had not been more alert. The march to the new camp continued, but by the time he arrived at the camp later in the day, his foot was swollen and seriously infected, and he was in agony. He was transferred by helicopter to Hue, where he was given massive doses of antibiotics and put in a room in the officers' quarters to recuperate. His career as an adviser, at least for this tour, was over. Despite the fact that he quickly recovered, the army did not want to send him back into the field. He had only a few months left in the country, and from now on, he would sit behind a desk at the headquarters of the First ARVN (Army of the Republic of Vietnam) Division, where he would work side by side with George Price.

The new assignment was, in Powell's words, "not comforting."[1] In the field, he had been immersed in day-to-day action. There was no overview of the war, no sense of how it was being fought. An American adviser had little time to think about the war's political goals or how decisions were being made. This real world of men struggling to survive against a determined enemy was, he soon found out, far removed from the world of those who thought about the war in bigger terms and who planned the politics and strategy of the conflict. Like most men in the field, Powell thought that the leaders in headquarters and in Washington were wise and were creating effective strategy.

That fantasy was soon exploded. Powell became aware that the United States, the most technologically advanced nation in the world, was putting its resources—men and equipment—into a struggle against an enemy who could win by dipping a stick in buffalo dung and hiding it in the ground. Powell had been removed from the field not by an expensive rifle or artillery piece, or by a multi-million-dollar jet, but by a primitive piece of wood, strategically placed by the hand of an invisible enemy.

Another thing he found not comforting were the methods being used to assess the success or failure of the American mission in Vietnam. There were a lot of people in headquarters using statistics to analyze the conflict. There was nothing wrong with statistics, but Powell understood that they could be manipulated to create certain impressions. There was also the issue of body counts—the estimate of how many of the enemy was killed in battle. As Powell came to realize, it was a difficult measure to come up with. The enemy carried off some of their dead, and the terrain in South Vietnam was dense and covered with vegetation. And then, even if body counts were reasonably accurate, what did they signify? The enemy seemed to have an inexhaustible supply of men that were willing to commit to fight against the South Vietnamese. Any observer in the field came to that conclusion without the aid of statistics and body counts. The conclusion that Powell came up with was easily stated: "Experts often possess more data than judgment."[2]

These uneasy feelings were reinforced at the very moment Powell left Vietnam. His departure date for the United States was scheduled for November 1963. On November 1, as Colin Powell was at Saigon's Tan Son Nhut Airport shipping his gear home, the government of South Vietnam was overthrown in a military coup. Powell could hear the gunfire as generals overthrew the government of South Vietnam's President Ngo Dinh

Diem and assassinated Diem and his brother. Although no one knew it at the time, the U.S. government had privately given the generals the go-ahead to overthrow Diem, although not to kill him.

It was a shocking event, and one that underscored the weakness of the South Vietnamese government and military. Colin Powell had his misgivings, but in 1963 he still believed, on the whole, in the value of the U.S. commitment in Vietnam. It was about stopping the spread of communism, which our government and people regarded as a worldwide threat. Communism was best stopped on the shores of Asia rather than on the coast of California. So the thinking of the time went.

Homecoming for any soldier who has been overseas for a long time is always an emotional moment, especially when the serviceman is about to meet a new baby he's never seen before. Michael Powell was now eight months old and had never seen his father. After the long flight from Vietnam, Colin Powell sat in the airport in Nashville waiting for his final connection to Birmingham. As he sat in the departure lounge, he heard the shattering news of the assassination of President John F. Kennedy in Dallas, Texas, earlier that day. It was November 22, 1963.

The national tragedy cast a pall on Powell's homecoming, but it did not dim the joy he felt on seeing Alma again and on meeting his firstborn child. For young Michael, of course, his father's arrival began a period of adjustment, as he learned to live in a universe that consisted now of two parents instead of one. After a few days in Birmingham, the family headed north to Queens for a reunion with Colin's parents. Then it was off to Fort Benning, Georgia, and the Infantry Officers Advanced Course, which would not begin, however, until August of 1964. In the meantime, Powell would have to find off-base housing for his family, and once again he faced the familiar problems confronting blacks in the South trying to find a suitable place to live. White residential areas of nearby Columbus were off limits to blacks, and after a frustrating search for a decent place to rent, Powell finally settled on a brick house owned by a Baptist minister in Phenix City, Alabama, just across the Georgia border. The house was fine, and it had a nice yard for Michael to play in. The reservation Powell had was the fact that Phenix City had a terrible reputation as a rough, crime-ridden town. Still, with so few options open to blacks, the minister's house, at $85 a month, seemed like a good deal.

As he waited for the advanced course to begin, Powell enrolled in what was known as the Pathfinder training. Pathfinders were an elite group of paratroopers whose mission was to jump into enemy territory before other airborne units in order to set up drop zones. The training was intense and exhausting. In addition to learning about landing zones, radio beacons, and all forms of navigation, the trainees made numerous jumps, most of them at night, and one even from a helicopter, which proved to be extremely dangerous.

Following the Pathfinder training, Powell once again received an unexpected assignment—he was posted to a group called the Infantry Board at Fort Benning. He was still awaiting the start of the advanced infantry course, and until it started, he was to become what amounted to a tester of army weapons and equipment. It seemed a strange posting for someone with combat experience and who had just finished the Pathfinder course. But as he was to discover, the Infantry Board turned out to be a good job. He got a chance to participate in a number of tests of diverse weapons systems and learned a lot about the politics that were involved in the selection of weapons and other military equipment. He was offered a job at the Board after he finished the training course, and he decided to accept. Powell had enjoyed the work, but in addition, a posting at Fort Benning would allow the family to stay together a while longer.

Finally, the advanced infantry course began in August 1964. It was a nine-month course, and during this time, Alma became pregnant with their second child. Powell remembered this period as one of the happiest in his life. He was with his family, he enjoyed the course, and he had a job awaiting him once the schooling was over. On April 16, 1965, Linda Powell was born at Martin Army Hospital. Powell relished the fact that he could be present for his daughter's birth, feeling the keen sense of loss by having missed Michael's birth two years before.

The following month, Powell graduated from the advanced infantry course—he placed number three in a class of 200. Powell was now positioned for bigger and better things, although at the time, he was content to return to the Infantry Board and provide a stable and loving environment for his wife and two children. But his career was moving fast. In May 1966, Powell received orders to become an instructor in the advanced infantry school. Before beginning teaching, Powell had to take an instructor's course. In later life, when he was a general, Powell would remember this course as providing him with the skills to stand with authority before a classroom full of young army officers. These skills proved valuable in later years as he dealt with the high stress of a Washington press conference.

In the 1960s, advanced infantry training was in great demand in the army. The pace of U.S. involvement in Vietnam had intensified after 1964, and the army needed fresh supplies of company- and field-grade officers. Powell, now a major, was one of a group of instructors helping the army create a fresh crop of officers to lead the American effort in Southeast Asia. From his instructor's vantage point, Powell understood all too well that he would have to go back to Vietnam eventually. All officers were bound to have at least two tours. And, as an army professional, he wanted to go. As a father and a husband, however, he did not want to leave his family behind. He worried about them, and he knew that they would miss him and be very anxious about his safety. The unspeakable was a possibility—he might be killed in action. But Powell was a career soldier, and Alma knew she had married a career soldier. So, on one level, they both understood that Powell's overseas duty was an unavoidable reality.

Anyone stationed at Fort Benning could not help being aware of the mounting casualties in Vietnam. As the center of army infantry training, Fort Benning's alumni were in the thick of the war. During his months as an instructor, Powell ran into an old buddy from his ROTC days and from Queens—Tony Mavroudis. Tony spent a lot of time with the family at Benning, and Alma and the children really liked his company. Tony had already been in Vietnam, but he volunteered for another tour. A couple of months after he left Benning, he was killed. Colin and Alma were devastated. The war was coming closer to home.

The only way that another tour in Vietnam might be deferred would be through additional educational training. In 1967, that opportunity arose— and it was one of the most important opportunities that Powell or any young army officer could achieve. In the spring of that year, Powell received the notice that he was assigned to the Command and General Staff College in Fort Leavenworth, Kansas.

The Command and General Staff College was another one of those requirements for any officer who aspired to the highest ranks in the army. Through its doors had passed some of the greatest names in army history, including Dwight D. Eisenhower and George Patton. The course was thirty-eight weeks long, and among its general objectives was to expose the army's future leaders to the big picture. Earlier training had tended to have a narrower focus. As an infantryman and a paratrooper, for example, Powell had studied technical details. But at the Command and General Staff College, he met people from all parts of the army—men who were engineers, others whose backgrounds were in armor and artillery, and in communications. The top leaders in the army had to deal with people from all these service branches. The Command and General Staff College was an early introduction to the army as a whole organization and not just a narrow area of specialization.

Powell once again excelled academically—a further boost to his already promising career. But he also enjoyed the environment of Fort

Leavenworth. For one thing, the course was attended by other African American officers; he and Alma enjoyed socializing with a wider circle of people. In addition, the college had many international students—officers from the military services of America's allies who came to the United States to attend the Command and General Staff College to study warfare and international relations. As it would turn out, Powell met many men he would encounter later in life when he was in Washington, both in the White House and in the Pentagon. He had begun to network on a national and international level.

At the beginning of 1968, the orders for Vietnam finally came through. Alma was stoic. She wished he didn't have to go, but he was an army officer—and one of the best and most promising army officers—and there was no question of his returning to battle. Colin and Alma decided that she and the children would return to Birmingham to live with her sister in a rented house about a mile or so from her parents' home. On the night before his departure, they went out to dinner at an expensive restaurant in Birmingham. Just a few short years before, that would not have been possible. Such a restaurant would have been segregated and off-limits to a black couple. But in 1968, public accommodations throughout the South were integrated, thanks to the Civil Rights Act of 1964. It was a quiet, intimate moment before his departure. The following day, July 21, 1968, Major Colin Powell set off for his second tour of duty in Vietnam.

Vietnam was a different place from the country Powell had first visited in 1962 and 1963. The 16,000 American advisers in-country in the early 1960s had grown to more than 500,000 troops involved in an active combat role for the United States. More than 30,000 American soldiers had been killed, and the war had created great conflict and debate in the United States. By 1968, antiwar sentiment in the country was strong and vocal. The war seemed an endless drain on American lives and treasure. No end was in sight, and we didn't seem to be fighting it to win. Scarcely a day went by when Americans didn't see an antiwar demonstration on TV, or hear another politician denounce the war. The daily images on TV of Americans fighting and dying in a far-off land, for what seemed to be an unclear objective, were turning more and more Americans against the conflict.

And then came the Tet offensive in February 1968. In this gigantic military assault, the North Vietnamese and Viet Cong staged surprise attacks on South Vietnamese cities throughout the country. The offensive was named after the Vietnamese holiday of Tet, a celebration of the lunar New Year. After ferocious battles, the enemy was driven back with enormous casualties. But for Americans, the lasting image was of a foe that despite years of American bombing and a half-million men was still able to mount a devastating attack all across the country. What was going on? On March 31, 1968, President Lyndon Johnson signaled a change in the war's direction. He halted the bombing of almost all of North Vietnam and announced he would not seek another term as president. The war had entered a new and uncertain phase.

Into this altered landscape, Colin Powell arrived again in Saigon. The elegant Asian city with the French feel was now swamped with American soldiers and refugees from the countryside. The black market economy flourished with American cigarettes and electronic equipment the most prized items. Prostitutes plied their trade in the many bars that catered to the American GIs. And Saigon air was more polluted as military jeeps, trucks, and other vehicles competed with the thousands of civilian motor scooters for space. The noise, the constant smell of burning garbage, the uncertain feeling about the war, especially after the Tet offensive—all this had changed Saigon into a sweaty and anxious city.

Once again, Powell would only be passing through the capital city of South Vietnam. This time, his assignment was in the northern part of the country, with the Third Battalion, First Infantry, Eleventh Infantry Brigade, part of the Americal Division. As the battalion's executive officer, Powell's job was to make sure that the unit had all the support it needed, from clothing to fuel to ammunition, among other things. The battalion was based at Duc Tho, near the city of Chu Lai. From time to time the base was attacked by mortars and rockets, but on the whole it was not considered a terribly dangerous location. One of Powell's responsibilities was to visit the battalion's field units—the fire support bases and landing zones on the front lines of combat. On these visits, which were made by helicopter, Powell saw the needs of his troops up front—and he saw death. Those killed in combat at these outer bases were helicoptered back to battalion headquarters for the final trip home to the United States.

The sight of the body bags moved him greatly and caused him to reflect even more on the war. Antiwar sentiment was at its peak in the United States, and in late October 1968, President Johnson halted all bombing of North Vietnam in an effort to push the peace talks that were taking place in Paris between the North and South Vietnamese and the United States. From Powell's perspective, as a military man, the bombing halt was something that could hurt the troops. He was there to do his job as a member of the military, and the care of his men was always paramount in his mind, although his caution and analytical abilities had led him more and more to question the wisdom of the war.

Shortly into his second tour in Vietnam, Powell was suddenly elevated to a new position. Major General Charles M. Gettys, the commanding general of the American Division, had met Powell briefly and was deeply impressed. He wanted him at division headquarters, and when the position as the head of G-3 became vacant (G-3 means planning and operations in army lingo), Gettys moved Powell into the slot—temporarily. The person originally promised the slot by Gettys had to finish another assignment and was not available to be head of G-3 for several months. The head of G-3, at a division level, is a position normally held by a lieutenant colonel, one rank higher than Powell. Powell had been bumped up over a number of other candidates of higher rank. Now instead of tending to a battalion's needs, he was responsible for the support for an entire 18,000-man division.

During his time at American Division headquarters, Powell again came face to face with death. In November 1968, General Gettys, Powell, and a number of other officers boarded the general's helicopter to head out into the field to inspect a large cache of enemy weapons captured a few days before. They were supposed to set down at a landing zone that had just been carved out of the jungle, a small patch that was nestled in the midst of jungle foliage. As the pilot attempted to set the helicopter down, Powell noticed that the rotor blades were perilously close to the trees. He shouted a warning to the pilot, but it was too late. The blades struck the trees and came immediately to a stop—which meant that the helicopter dropped to the ground with a tremendous thud. Everyone on board was injured, and Powell suffered a broken ankle. Despite his wounds, Powell helped the more seriously injured out of the wreckage. It had been a nerve-racking close call.

In January 1969, Powell was able to get away from Vietnam for a brief period of R & R (rest and recuperation). R & R was available to all servicemen in Vietnam, and after the helicopter crash, Powell welcomed the opportunity to fly to Hawaii, where he would spend a delightful week with Alma and the two children, who had flown there from Birmingham. The family spent hours together on the beach and just enjoyed whatever fleeting moments they were able to grab. A week later, Powell was on his way back to Vietnam to complete the final six months of his tour of duty.

The last half of his Vietnam service went by uneventfully. During this time, the army began to investigate an incident that had occurred in March of 1968; three months before Powell arrived back in Vietnam. At that time, a unit of the Eleventh Infantry Brigade committed a terrible atrocity, shooting more than 300 Vietnamese civilians—men, women, and children—in what became known as the infamous My Lai massacre. In 1969 the leader of the unit, Lieutenant William Calley, was convicted of murder and sentenced to life in prison, a sentence that was later commuted by President Richard M. Nixon.

Although My Lai had occurred before Powell joined the Eleventh Infantry Brigade, it greatly disturbed Powell. Americans were good people. American servicemen were dedicated, honorable young men. How could something like this happen, where ordinary men would line up women and children in a ditch and mow them down with machine-gun fire? There were no easy answers to these questions, but Powell came away from Vietnam with opinions and ideas that would guide him throughout the rest of his military and diplomatic career. In his opinion, the American government had lied to the people about the war from the outset. The country's political leaders deceived themselves and the public into believing that the war was going well, hiding behind such phony statistics like body counts. All the while, the war, in his view, was not winnable politically. The North Vietnamese were willing to take incredible casualties, as Tet had demonstrated, in order to win the conflict and unite their country. They could outwait the United States.

Moreover, the U.S. government was also not willing to go all the way to win the war militarily. The draft system had numerous loopholes that allowed students and other well-connected people to get out of serving, thus assuring that the bulk of infantry soldiers thrown into conflict were from the poorer segments of society—with many being men of color. This, according to Powell, was "an antidemocratic disgrace."[3] In a memorable passage in his autobiography, Powell summarized the philosophy that crystallized as a result of his second tour in Vietnam:

War should be the politics of last resort. And when we go to war, we should have a purpose that our people understand and support; we should mobilize the country's resources to fulfill that mission and then go in to win. In Vietnam, we had entered into a half-hearted half-war, with much of the nation opposed or indifferent, while a small fraction carried the burden.[4]

Powell's heart broke for the average soldier, the kid who carried the burden and had, in effect, been betrayed by the political leaders in Washington. Later, when Powell was in charge of all the U.S. military, he would steadfastly adhere to the lessons learned in Vietnam, would urge them on the political leaders he served, and would apply them to the crises he faced.

In July 1969 he was headed home—to Alma and the children, to his parents, and to a new chapter in his life as a student in the nation's capital.

NOTES

1. Powell, *My American Journey*, p. 97.
2. Ibid., p. 99.
3. Ibid., p. 144.
4. Ibid., p. 143.

Chapter 5

THE YOUNG COMMANDER: MOVING UP IN THE ARMY AND GOVERNMENT

When he was studying at the Command and General Staff College at Fort Leavenworth, Colin Powell thought about going to graduate school at a civilian university for an advanced degree. The army allowed officers to study for master's degree and Ph.D., and Powell intended to take advantage of this policy. In his last month in Vietnam, he was accepted at the School of Government and Business Administration at the George Washington University (GWU) in Washington, D.C. Powell could now live almost like a civilian—out of uniform, attending classes during the week, and living off post—which meant, of course, that he could be with his family every day. Shortly before school began, Alma and Colin bought their first house, in Dale City, Virginia, a short commute from the nation's capital.

As enjoyable as it was to be a civilian again, for however long, Powell soon discovered that graduate school was a challenge. At the age of 32, he was the oldest student in his class. The degree he was seeking, an MBA (master of business administration) in data processing, required intensive work, and for a time, Powell wondered if he would be able to finish the course. He later modestly said that he was surprised that he did, but in fact he was a top student and received his degree with high honors.

During his time at GWU, Powell became a father for the third time. On May 20, 1970, another baby girl, Annemarie, joined the Powell family. As a graduate student, Powell had a lot of free time and flexible hours, so it gave him the welcome opportunity to spend a lot of time with Annemarie—a pleasure he had not had when Michael was born. He happily played with his new daughter and walked her around the neighborhood, proudly showing her off to neighbors.

Two months after Annemarie's birth, Powell was promoted to the rank of lieutenant colonel. The army was giving him a vote of confidence with the advancement. At the age of 33, he was only a rank away from one-star general. Graduate school had been an exciting challenge, but when he received his MBA in 1971, Powell decided that that was enough schooling. One adviser had suggested that he continue on to get his doctorate, but Powell knew what he wanted: he was a soldier, and he wanted to get back to active service.

The next assignment moved Powell to the very center of military power in the United States. He was assigned to the office of the assistant vice chief of staff of the Army and would be based at the Pentagon. The assistant vice chief, Lieutenant General William E. DePuy, was an intense three-star general who was also a Vietnam veteran. DePuy enjoyed a reputation as a terrifying man who demanded the utmost from his subordinates and was totally lacking in patience or sympathy if anyone failed to perform. Those not living up to his exacting standards were fired. Despite the cranky exterior, DePuy was in fact a true reformer, an officer impatient with the inefficiencies, old-boy networks, and lies that had been told to make it seem that the Vietnam War was going well. His role as vice chief of staff was to come up with genuine reforms for the post-Vietnam Army, and Powell was to be part of the group devising future policies. Powell's MBA was in computers and data processing, but he was assigned broader duties that went beyond his job description.

Working in a Pentagon job, like going to GWU, allowed Powell to enjoy an almost-civilian lifestyle. He and his family lived off base, and they took pleasure in the advantages that life in or near a big city offered. The Powells tended to socialize with other army people, and during the Pentagon period Colin became involved with a kind of club made up of African American officers dedicated to befriending, encouraging, and supporting the careers of young black officers in the army. The group called themselves "the Rocks," a name that derived from Brigadier General Roscoe "Rock" Cartwright, an African American officer. The group used Cartwright's nickname to honor him and his wife. Shortly before Powell came to Washington, General and Mrs. Cartwright had been killed in a plane crash. The Rocks met for dinner and drinks at each other's homes on weekends, but their main mission was to visit black colleges to encourage young African Americans to join the ROTC. Each year they gave an award to the outstanding ROTC cadet at a black college. For Powell, the

Rocks were part of a historic tradition in the African American community—blacks taking care of other blacks.

The Pentagon assignment turned out to be another transitional position. Working in DePuy's office was a superb job, but others in the Army singled out Powell for a position he had never given a moment's thought to. In November 1971, the office of the Infantry Branch suggested to Powell that he apply for a position as a White House Fellow. He had never heard of this position, and at first didn't even realize that he was being ordered to apply for it. He soon learned, however, that the Secretary of Defense, Melvin Laird, was unhappy that too few military people were applying to be White House Fellows. The army, like the other military branches, was combing through its ranks for qualified candidates to meet the secretary's wishes and to get more military personnel into this prestigious job.

But what was a White House Fellow? The program had been established a few years earlier during the administration of President Lyndon B. Johnson. White House Fellows were young people of achievement from the world of business, education, government, and the military who were chosen to work in a variety of positions in Washington for a period of one year, during which time they would see how the government worked and how policy was made. Powell was very skeptical about applying to be a White House Fellow, especially since he was enjoying working for General DePuy. But an order was an order.

The interview process was grueling. On his application, Powell was asked why he wanted to be a White House Fellow. He really didn't, but he thought for a while, then realized that in the wake of the Vietnam War, a large portion of the American population had negative views of the military, a development that Powell felt was both tragic and unhealthy for a democracy. In the 1960s and early 1970s, ROTC membership at CCNY had declined to a handful of participants, and in 1972, the school's program was abolished altogether. Kids who joined ROTC were hassled for being warmongers and were considered very uncool.

Powell was heartbroken by this and thought that his participation as a White House Fellow could help demonstrate the importance of the military and the good qualities of the men and women who joined it. After a series of intensive interviews, Powell received notice that he had been accepted as a White House Fellow for the year 1972–1973. He was distinctly of two minds about the opportunity. On the one hand, it would expose him to the highest levels of the U.S. government and allow him to meet influential people from government and civilian life. And it would permit him to remain in Washington for another year. On the other hand, he would be leaving a particularly important office in the Defense Department and would be off on yet another tangent for at least a year.

Powell decided that he wanted to spend his time as a White House Fellow at the Office of Management and Budget (OMB). This was the main agency responsible for shaping the president's budget. It was, in short, one of the most important power centers in the federal government. Powell interviewed for a slot at the OMB with Frank Carlucci, who was the deputy director. Carlucci reported to Caspar Weinberger, the director of OMB. Both Weinberger and Carlucci would later become secretaries of defense in the administration of President Ronald Reagan in the 1980s. They proved to be important men in Powell's career. In his early months at OMB, he also got to know the major deputies in all the cabinet departments. He would soon come to understand that the deputies and especially the civil service—which stayed on in government from one administration to another—were almost always the people who ran the departments and who knew how to get things done. This was another valuable lesson in working with and controlling large bureaucratic organizations.

Within a few months of Powell's arrival at OMB, Weinberger and Carlucci went on to other assignments. Fred Malek, a dynamic man who taught Powell many things about government, replaced Carlucci as deputy director. Malek had been one of the people who had interviewed Powell for the White House Fellow position, and after he was installed as deputy director at OMB, he asked Powell to be his assistant. Malek's main objective at OMB was to gain some control over the vast federal bureaucracy for President Richard Nixon. He planned to do this by installing people loyal to him and to President Nixon in the major cabinet departments at the level of assistant or deputy secretaries. The cabinet officers who headed each department could appear on TV and speak to the public, but Malek's people would really run the department and carry out the wishes of President Nixon. Malek was bold and brazen enough to try to plant his people in the federal bureaucracy. In the end, however, President Nixon was forced to resign in 1974 because of the Watergate scandal, and the plan he and Malek had concocted was never enacted. Powell realized that this was probably for the good, since too much power in the hands of any president could be dangerous. But he also learned an important lesson from Malek's way of operating in government. As he later stated, "You don't know what you can get away with until you try."[1]

White House Fellows had the opportunity to travel abroad to learn about government in foreign countries. In early 1973, Powell left on a major trip with other White House Fellows. It was to a country that would figure prominently in his later career as a top officer and a diplomat—the Soviet Union. In 1973, the Soviet Union and the United States were enjoying relatively good relations after years of tension and rivalry.

In 1972, President Nixon, in a major shift in U.S. foreign policy, signed an arms-limitation treaty with the Soviets, inaugurating a period known as *détente*. Nixon traveled to Moscow in June 1972 to sign the treaty. The agreement, which limited ballistic missiles, represented an effort to lower the heat and reduce the tensions between the two powers, whose nuclear arsenals had the potential to wipe out the entire world.

Thus, when Colin Powell arrived in the Soviet Union in 1973, in the frigid Siberian city of Khabarovsk, U.S.-Soviet relations were the best they had been in 30 years. But old habits died hard. Unlike the United States, where both citizens and foreign visitors are free to travel around on their own to almost anywhere in the country, the Soviet Union assigned guides to accompany foreigners. These so-called guides were actually members of the Soviet security services, and their job was to keep an eye on the foreigners and make sure that they did not wander off on their own—and especially not have unauthorized contacts with ordinary Russians. On one of his first nights in the country, Powell and a colleague thought they would wander and visit a pub where ordinary Russians gathered. Within minutes of arriving at the pub, they were followed in by their official guides, who suggested that they not visit the tavern and might like to return to their hotel. They got the message and left.

From Khabarovsk, the Americans boarded the Trans-Siberian railroad for the trip westward. The Soviet Union is so vast that after three solid days of train travel, they were still in Siberia! Their destination was the city of Irkutsk, on Lake Baikal, in central Russia. When he traveled along the shores of Lake Baikal, the largest inland freshwater lake in Europe and Asia, Powell noticed the terrible pollution. After the Russian Revolution in 1917 and the coming to power of communism, the Soviet government had plunged the country into an orgy of industrialization. Factories by the thousands were built, with little thought given to the impact of this rapid industrializing on the ecology of the nation. Now, after years of reckless expansion, aging, rusty factories belched black smoke into the air over Lake Baikal, and industrial wastes were routinely dumped into its waters. Lake Baikal eventually became an ecological disaster, its fish stock destroyed and its beauty marred by air and water pollution. It was a disturbing sight, one that helped Powell understand more about the nature of the Soviet regime and of life in the Soviet Union.

The trip to the Soviet Union taught Powell the difference between reading and studying about the Soviet Union and experiencing it first-hand. Here was the enemy he had been taught about as a young officer, the opponents he had faced across the Iron Curtain in Europe. Yet, the trip had also given him an overwhelming awareness that the Russian people were just like people all over the world. They were human beings, ordinary people just like Americans. They worked hard and they wanted the best in life for their children. They were good and courageous people. Politics and war were not so simple. The enemy was also made up of real people, and a leader needed to keep these realities in the forefront of his mind.

After a few months back in the states, the White House Fellows were off on their second foreign trip. This time, it was to the other big power that had been a traditional adversary of the United States—China. The early 1970s was the beginning of a new era in relations between the United States and the People's Republic of China. During World War II, the United States had supported the government of the Chinese Nationalist leader Chiang Kai-shek in its fight against the Japanese invaders. After the war, Chiang's government, which was pro-American but weak and corrupt, became embroiled in a civil war with the communists led by Mao Tse-tung. After four years of fighting, Mao's forces won, and all mainland China became communist. Chiang and the Nationalist government fled to the nearby island of Taiwan and set up their regime. The United States recognized the Chiang government for the next 20 years. During the war in Vietnam, the United States considered communist China to be an ally of the North Vietnamese—which they were to some degree, although the Vietnamese and Chinese had a long history of animosity toward each other.

In the early 1970s, all this changed. It had to. Communist China was one of the largest countries in the world. The United States could no longer ignore this titan among nations, nor could the Chinese—who desired to modernize their economy—afford to be an enemy of the wealthy United States, which promised to be a huge market for their products.

In 1971, President Richard Nixon stunned the world by announcing that he would visit communist China in February 1972. This historic visit marked a turning point in Chinese-American relations, the first effort on the part of both countries to put more than 30 years of hostility behind them and work at building a new relationship. It was to this China—scarcely 18 months after Nixon's historic visit—that Colin Powell journeyed in 1973. He and his party entered China through the historic southern city of Canton. In contrast to the Soviets, the Chinese on first glance seemed less rigid and paranoid, at least in their day-to-day contacts with Westerners. Canton was an immaculate city; through its streets millions of people pedaled around on their bicycles, the favorite mode of transportation for the Chinese, who at this stage in their development did not have many privately owned automobiles. Although seemingly relaxed in their dealings with foreigners, the Chinese were no less under the influence of their communist party than were the Soviets. Everyone Powell spoke with expressed total devotion to Mao and his ideals. It seemed a bizarre sentiment, given that in the early 1970s China was still emerging from a convulsive period known as the "Cultural Revolution," in which millions of people were purged from the party and their jobs and sometimes sent to the countryside to do forced labor. People in once-respected jobs were publicly humiliated. Professors were sometimes forced to wear dunce caps in front of their students and to confess their crimes. Many people were executed, others committed suicide, and millions of lives were ruined or changed forever. The Chinese communists were equally interested as their Soviet counterparts in controlling the actions and thoughts of their citizens.

But the China of 1973 was struggling past this period. It was interested in Western technology and investment, and the contacts that began with President Nixon's visit were beginning to bear fruit. China gave Powell an opportunity to observe up close the most powerful nation in mainland Asia. He toured the renowned historic sites such as the Great Wall and the Forbidden City and—more important—got a chance to meet with ordinary people as well as government officials. Powell came away deeply impressed by the Chinese people, who through years of suffering were able to look optimistically toward their future and work hard to achieve a better and more prosperous society. But, as in the Soviet Union, Powell was disturbed by the kinds of dictatorial control the Chinese government exercised over its people's daily lives and thoughts. As a military man, Powell had seen the world—from the vantage point of a soldier on active duty. As a White House Fellow, he saw the two most powerful adversaries of the United States as an honored guest, an official of the U.S. government.

After the China trip, it was just a matter of a couple of months before the White House fellowship was over. Powell really wanted to get back to the army. Years later, he would understand how important the White House detour had been in terms of exposure to governments, here and abroad, and for networking with people he would meet up with again later in government. But in 1973, what he really wanted was to command a battalion. Lieutenant colonels commanded battalion-level units, and Powell needed this experience. His desire to leave the government and cross the Potomac and go back to the Pentagon was also reinforced by the Watergate scandal, which was breaking open all through 1973 and which would lead to the resignation of President Nixon the following year. As Powell later said, the Nixon administration did not look like a "particularly seaworthy vessel."[2]

Getting a good battalion command, however, was not that easy. Unlike today, in the early 1970s many high-ranking positions in the Army were filled through connections to the old-boy network: A choice assignment was often a matter of whom you knew and the nature of the network of friendships you had built up over the years. Powell certainly had many friends and was considered a rising star, but he had also taken a lot of detours in the course of his career, the latest being the White House fellowship. As it turned out, he was offered a battalion command—not a choice one in the States or in Europe, but in Korea. He needed to take this command, but it was not easy breaking the news to Alma. Families could not accompany officers to Korea, so it would mean another yearlong separation. Alma took the news in good spirit, but it was painful for all involved—Colin, Alma, and the children. An army officer always faced the prospect of an overseas assignment without his family. It never got easier, but it was part of the army life.

The command Powell was offered was the First Battalion, Thirty-second Infantry, of the Second Infantry Division—a unit of the Eighth Army in Korea. This unit was known as the "Queen's Own Buccaneers," a name it had borne since its founding in Hawaii in the 1890s. At that time, Hawaii was not a U.S. state but was ruled by the Hawaiian royal family headed by Queen Liliuokalani. The "Bucs" were named to honor her.

The United States had been in Korea since the early 1950s. In June 1950, the communist government of North Korea, at the instigation of China and the Soviet Union, invaded South Korea, which was a non-communist state allied with the United States. The United States and the United Nations sent troops to Korea to fight the North Koreans. The resulting conflict—the Korean War—lasted from 1950 until 1953, when an armistice was agreed upon to end the fighting and leave the border between North and South Korea basically the same as it had been before the war. The United States also left a large body of troops in South Korea to protect that country from any future invasion. After 1953, there was no more war, but by the time Colin Powell arrived there in the early 1970s, the U.S. forces still numbered in the tens of thousands. Americans sulting from these kinds of absences was extremely high. Although AWOLs were a problem, from Powell's perspective they were preferable in many ways to the troops going to prostitutes (having one girlfriend was probably safer than having sex with many), resulting in high levels of venereal disease.

Powell also had to deal with racial tensions, which were strained, in the Second Division. Disputes would often erupt over seemingly unimportant matters, for example, music. Black soldiers often wanted to hear soul and the music of black performers. White soldiers would sometimes prefer rock and country. As unbelievable as it might sound, fights erupted on base, but the tensions were really rooted in the racial divide that was an unpleasant import from life back in the United States. Racial unrest also spilled over into the bars in Tong Du Chon that catered to the Americans. There were black bars and white bars, and tensions between them were high. Emerson and Powell made a concerted effort to lower the tensions. The merchants of Tong Du Chon were told in no uncertain terms that segregated bars would not be tolerated. In addition, soldiers were encouraged to come forward with their problems and talk to the chaplain or an officer. General Emerson tolerated no racial bias whatsoever and he dismissed anyone who expressed racist ideas or acted in a biased manner.

Gradually, morale improved and racial tensions lessened, thanks to the strong and clear leadership of Emerson and Powell. Powell also learned some important lessons that he later implemented when he was in higher office. The U.S. forces in Korea were made up of many draftees. By contrast, a professional army would more likely enjoy higher morale because its members were there by choice. In the army of the 1950s, many humiliating practices from the past had been retained—such as kitchen patrol (KP), an odious task that put a soldier in the kitchen washing heavy pots and pans for 18 hours on end. There was no reason to retain this practice when civilians could be hired and paid a salary to be kitchen workers. Another archaic humiliation was the practice of screaming at lower-ranked soldiers and even using certain kinds of physical abuse—all of which, Powell came to believe, distracted from the professionalism the army was seeking and from the morale that was absolutely essential for the services to be a top fighting force.

Vietnam was a lesson in the military-in-action in the 1960s. After the second Vietnam tour, Powell had been exposed to some of the headiest assignments the army could offer. It was a long way from ROTC to the corridors of power in Washington. Korea, however, was a lesson in day-to-day reality in the modern army when it was not at war. Here Powell saw morale and discipline problems, racial unrest, and the boredom that can

seemed to be in Korea for the long run—and this fact, as it turned out, w
a reality that affected Powell as a battalion commander. Troops station
in a foreign country in which there was no war faced many challenges, tl
main one being the troubles they could get into because of boredom ai
homesickness. The resulting problems with discipline and morale we
not unlike those Powell had seen in Germany in the 1950s.

The commander of the Second Division was Major General Henry
Emerson, nicknamed "the Gunfighter," a man who drove his men ha
but was fair and honorable. Emerson was a man of loudly expressed e
thusiasms. Staff meetings would usually begin calmly, but by the time tl
general had gotten wound up, his fist would be pounding the table as l
urged his officers on to excellence. The same would occur when he a
dressed the troops. A speech that began quietly usually ended with Eme
son yelling that if the North Koreans ever attacked again, the Unit
States would kick their asses.[3] The troops were so delighted with Eme
son's performance that they would shout "Go, Gunfighter, go!" The nan
stuck.

Korea was cold in the winter—bitterly cold. Even a high-ranking of
cer like Powell had to live in a freezing tin hut with a desk, a bed, a cha
and a heater that gave off smoky fumes. Camp Casey, the home base of tl
Second Division, was about an hour north of the South Korean capital
Seoul. The nearest town to the base was named Tong Du Chon. Lil
countless other such towns around the world—towns situated in tl
shadow of an American military base—Tong Du Chon existed to ser
the American military. The Americans meant income, far more mon
than the average Korean, at the time, could earn in such a small tow
Tailors would make any item of clothing for a soldier overnight, and for
few dollars. Artists would take an ordinary photograph of a soldier's fai
ily and make an oil painting of the picture. Even if the people in the pi
ture ended up looking ethnically Korean, it was the thought that counte
Vendors on Tong Du Chon's narrow alleys sold ashtrays, plates, candl
sticks, and any number of brass and metal items, many of them made fro
discarded American shells fired during exercises near Camp Casey.

Two of the most important items provided by the enterprising me
chants of Tong Du Chon were alcohol and women. A young soldier cou
rent a small apartment in town for about $180 a month. It was a gre
deal. With the apartment came a girl who would clean house, do laundr
and—most important—be a live-in girlfriend. The soldier, of cours
could not stay long at the apartment, perhaps making an overnight vis
from time to time. The men who did this were often written up for bein
absent without leave (AWOL), and the number of short-term AWOLs r

sap a unit's strength; and he also came to appreciate ways in which an army needed to be modernized. An all-volunteer force could not afford to be an unappealing place if the government wanted people to make their life careers in the military. In addition, more and more women were enlisting; a fact that created different needs and considerations as the army looked to its future role in the defense of the nation.

But now it was time for Powell to leave Korea, to return to his family in the States. His parting evaluation from Gunfighter was glowing. This man, Emerson wrote, should be a general. Powell later said that the tour in Korea helped him realize that more than anything else he wanted to command an infantry unit. He would end up commanding, but not in quite the way he had envisioned.

NOTES

1. Powell, *My American Journey*, p. 162.
2. Ibid., p. 171.
3. Ibid., p. 174.

Chapter 6

AN UNCONVENTIONAL CAREER: THE INNER CIRCLES OF GOVERNMENT

Just before Colin Powell left Korea in September 1974, Alma wrote to him and made a prediction about their future. She was optimistic, perhaps because their yearlong absence from each other was about to end. At the close of her letter, Alma said that something big and exciting will happen.[1] Powell himself wasn't so sure that anything big and exciting was on the horizon, because—once again—he had been selected for a special assignment out of the command structure of the army. And this time, it was another educational detour. Powell was chosen to attend what is often called the "Harvard University" of military schools—the prestigious National War College at Fort McNair, in Washington, D.C. This special school was attended by the best and the brightest, not only from all the military services but also from the State Department, the Central Intelligence Agency (CIA), and the U.S. Information Agency. Lecturers included some of the top people in government and the military. There were no tests; those who attended were exposed to the great classic and contemporary military thinkers and also had the opportunity to mingle with and get to know other bright people on their way up in government and the services.

The course started in August 1975. Between the fall of 1974 and the summer of 1975, Powell worked temporarily at the Pentagon, where he served on an interservice board assigned to create a report for Congress on the future manpower needs of all branches of the military. It was Powell's first exposure to how the different services interact and guard their respective turfs. The army, navy, air force, and marines each fought for its slice of the budgetary pie, at the expense of the other branches if necessary. When Powell was the Chairman of the Joint Chiefs of Staff in the 1990s, these were exactly the kind of concerns he would have to deal with: compromising and making sure each branch of the military had its needs met, while at the same time the overall defense of the nation was kept at its highest level.

Shortly after the course at the National War College began, Powell was promoted to full colonel. The next rank up was brigadier general, and although the competition was now getting extremely tight, Powell's chances looked good for further advancement. As the term ended, Powell was informed that he would take command of the Second Brigade of the 101st Airborne Division in Fort Campbell, Kentucky. A brigade, which is commanded by a full colonel, consists of three battalions. This command was exactly the kind of challenge Powell welcomed.

The 101st Airborne, known as the "Screaming Eagles," was a distinguished unit founded in 1942. It had seen some of the fiercest action in World War II, including parachuting into France during the Normandy invasion in June 1944. By the 1970s, the 101st was no longer a parachute unit but specialized in the movement of infantry by helicopter. This helicopter-infantry combination made the 101st unique. Its commander was Major General John Wickham, a small, intense man who had been severely wounded in Vietnam and who was fiercely dedicated to the mission of the 101st.

Two of Powell's three battalions needed to be brought up to speed. They were not performing well, and Powell was told immediately by Wickham that the battalions had to improve. Powell realized he would have to push the men—hard. One way he chose was to require that everyone qualify in air assault school. Since Powell's units were infantry, they were not required to learn air assault techniques, which were physically demanding and at times even dangerous. But Powell realized what a good impression this would make on Wickham and other division leaders, so everyone in the unit—no exceptions—was required to learn air assault. Many of the men were furious, and an occasional officer even transferred out of the Second Brigade rather than go through the strenuous training. In the end, however, every man passed the course, and the Brigade's performance—and prestige—rose.

When he was not working, life on the base at Fort Campbell was comfortable for Alma and the children. The kids were growing up—Michael was a young teenager, and the girls were growing up fast. They were all good students, and their parents were justly proud of their accomplishments. There was no episcopal congregation on base, so Alma and Colin helped round up the few Episcopalians who were there and founded an

episcopal worship group. Alma reached out to other people at Fort Campbell by becoming involved in all kinds of volunteer work. Powell hoped
that he would eventually be promoted to the position of chief of staff of
the 101st Division. But, as in the past, a call came from Washington.

On January 20, 1977, Jimmy Carter was sworn in as the thirty-ninth
President of the United States. In that month, Powell was summoned by
Carter's national security adviser, Zbigniew Brzezinski, for an interview.
Brzezinski had heard good things about Powell, who was known in the executive through his Pentagon and White House fellowship service. He
wanted Powell to join the National Security Council (NSC) as director of
the military staff. The NSC advises the president on national security issues. As such, it is a key center of power, since national security information from all the cabinet departments goes through the NSC for evaluation
before it is sent to the president. Brzezinski really wanted Powell and put
the pressure on for him to join the administration. But Powell resisted.
He just wanted to be an army commander and was tired of these recur-
ring detours into government. After politely turning down the offer, he
returned to Kentucky, only to discover that he would not be getting the
chief of staff job he had craved. Wickham correctly predicted Powell's
future. He told him that he would not have a conventional career in the
Army, and that the Carter administration would soon be back with another job offer.

How right he was. In May 1977, Brzezinski called again and offered
Powell another job at the NSC. At the same time, Powell also received a
call from the Pentagon, where he was offered a job on the staff of John
Kester, a special assistant to Secretary of Defense Harold Brown. Powell,
disappointed in not getting the chief of staff job at the 101st, decided to
accept the Pentagon position. Kester was a shrewd political operator who
knew how to acquire power and influence. More important, he was totally
unafraid (or impressed by) high-ranking military officers. Every document
that went to Secretary Brown had to go through Kester's hand, and this
fact alone gave him enormous power. No matter who you were, if you
wanted to get Harold Brown's ear, you had to get past Kester. If Kester didn't
like you, your telephone calls might go unanswered, or your memos to
Harold Brown might get lost. Kester also got a hand on high-level promotions and instituted a change that infuriated some of the generals.
Army tradition had allowed high-ranking generals the privilege of nam-
ing candidates for certain promotions. A four-star general, for example,
might recommend someone in his unit for promotion to three stars.
Kester, with Brown's approval, now required that at least two names be
submitted for a promotion and that the Secretary of Defense make the

final choice. Because Powell was a man in uniform, the generals often complained to him about Kester—but to no avail. He was able to serve as a shoulder to cry on, but he could do little to change the way Kester and Brown ran their office. It was again one of those lessons in how to survive and prosper in a large bureaucracy.

During his time in Kester's office, Powell suffered a personal tragedy. After several months of declining health, Luther Powell died on April 29, 1978. During his father's final illness, Powell was able to visit him on weekends, flying up to New York on the Washington–LaGuardia shuttle. His father's death was a terrible blow for Colin. Luther had always been a self-assured, strong, and independent man. In his final months, he was stricken with cancer and became an invalid—a terrible decline that caused Powell enormous grief.

Powell's father, unfortunately, did not live to see Colin's promotion to brigadier general. Although not unexpected, the promotion put Powell into the top elite of the army and promised a career that could have even greater rewards. The formal promotion ceremony was held on June 1, 1979, in Harold Brown's private dining room at the Pentagon. Alma and the children, Powell's mother, and numerous aunts, uncles, and cousins were present to see the ROTC candidate from the Bronx have the secretary of defense pin a silver star on his shoulder. Powell was not the first African American to become a general, but, at 42, he was the youngest general on service in the army.

While on service at the Pentagon, Powell met another person who would play an important role in his career. Charles Duncan was Deputy Defense Secretary immediately under Harold Brown. He was Kester's immediate boss. Duncan and Powell became close friends and played racquetball together to relax. In 1979, President Carter chose Duncan to be Secretary of Energy. Duncan immediately asked Powell to join him at the Energy Department. Of all the detours he had faced in the past, a move to the Energy Department was one that was farthest removed from the army. Although he was reluctant to accept, Powell decided to follow his friend, but for a short time only. In his two and one-half months at Energy, Powell helped Duncan organize his office. Once that task was complete, Powell hoped to return to a command. But the old script was still in place. Instead of a command, Powell was returned to the Pentagon, this time as the military assistant to Duncan's successor, W. Graham Claytor Jr.

Powell's time in Claytor's office coincided with one of the most trying times in recent American history—and one that was severely damaging to the morale of the military. In November 1979, more than 50 American Foreign Service and military personnel working at the U.S. embassy in Teheran, Iran, were taken hostage with the support of the revolutionary Muslim Iranian government. The Iranians were furious with the United States for its support of Iran's previous leader, Shah Reza Pahlavi, who had fled the country in January 1979 and by 1980 was seeking treatment for terminal cancer in the United States. By April of 1980 President Carter, frustrated with the never-ending crisis that was sapping his popularity ratings in an election year, authorized a highly risky rescue mission using eight helicopters and six C-130 transport aircraft. The mission ended in disaster in the Iranian desert when one of the helicopters collided with one of the planes. Eight Americans were killed, the rescue was scrapped, and Carter and the American military were humiliated. Powell applauded the bravery of the men who had risked so much to try to save their fellow Americans captives in Iran. But he was also angry at the poor planning, the lack of coordination, and the high risk involved in the operation in the first place. The Iran rescue mission reinforced Powell's cautious approach to the use of force. More than ever before, he came to believe that force should be used only when there is a clearly defined political and military goal and when the mission is winnable. In addition, the troops must always be given total and complete support so they can achieve their goals. All these had been lacking in the Iran operation.

The failed rescue also led Powell to have a change of heart about Jimmy Carter. He had voted for Carter, a pro–civil rights southern Democrat, when he ran for president in 1976. But now Powell felt he could no longer support Carter for reelection and that the country needed a change. In November 1980, Powell cast his ballot for the Republican, Ronald Reagan, who won in a landslide. Reagan's victory meant that many people Powell had met in the early 1970s would be returning to government. As a military man stationed at the Pentagon, Powell was naturally anxious to find out who would be the new Secretary of Defense. Reagan announced that it would be Caspar Weinberger, and that his Deputy Defense Secretary would be Frank Carlucci. Weinberger, a tough and brilliant man, had the nickname "Cap the Knife" because of his reputation as a fearless budget cutter. But Weinberger, like Reagan, was determined to increase military spending in order to beef up the military, which he believed had declined during the Carter years. The first Defense budget under Weinberger called for an 11 percent increase in spending— a dramatic change welcomed by the professional military, especially because much of the spending went to bread-and-butter items such as increased wages, improved housing, training, better dental care, and the like.

Weinberger was also curious why many high-ranking military aides, such as Powell, went to work wearing civilian clothes. When he was told that the previous administration did not want to draw attention to the number of uniformed personnel in these positions, Weinberger became angry. He did not want military people to have to hide in civilian clothes—it sent the wrong message to the services and to the country. The order went out—wear your uniform to work. Powell gladly reverted to the uniform he was so proud to wear.

Carlucci replaced Graham Claytor. He remembered Powell from the OMB and immediately asked him to remain for a short time as his military assistant. Carlucci liked Powell so much that he was hoping to move him into a civilian position at the Pentagon. The Secretary of the Army, John Marsh, even suggested that Powell resign from active duty to assume the civilian position of Undersecretary of the Army. This is something Powell absolutely did not want to do. Instead, he pressed Carlucci for a new assignment in the army. In the spring of 1981, Powell was appointed assistant division commander for operations and training of the Fourth Infantry Division (Mechanized), located at Fort Carson, Colorado.

It seemed like an ideal posting. Before Powell and his family uprooted themselves for the trip west, however, he was warned that the job might not be so enjoyable. The problem: the Fourth Infantry's commander, Major General John W. Hudachek, the man who would be Powell's immediate superior. Hudachek and his wife, Ann, had reputations for being difficult people to work with. Hudachek, a man of few words and no smiles, ran the division, and his wife ran the other wives. But Powell was not intimidated. He had worked in the halls of the Pentagon and met all kinds of strong personalities both on the civilian and the military side. He refused to believe that he couldn't get along with Hudachek.

Fort Carson was located south of Colorado Springs in the foothills of the beautiful Rocky Mountains. It was quite a different setting from all the familiar places Colin and Alma had visited east of the Mississippi. Powell's new job would focus on division training. A mechanized division is basically a tank division. Although Powell was an infantryman, he felt he could learn quickly about tanks. Shortly after his arrival at Fort Carson, he made his first attempt to drive an M-60A1 tank. Unfortunately, at one point as the tank sank into a depression, Powell lowered its gun tube downward, the exact movement that should never have been made under such circumstances—when a tank sinks into a hole, the gun tube should be raised. The gun tube made a sickening scraping sound on the ground. Luckily, the tank was not seriously damaged, and Powell was suitably humbled and more careful the next time he drove. But he had shown his determination to learn what his men and his unit were all about, even if he stumbled.

For the Powell family, Fort Carson was another big adjustment. Michael was off to college. Although he had been accepted at West Point, he decided to attend the College of William and Mary in Virginia and did not join the family in Colorado. Linda transferred to a local high school, where she entered her third year, and Annemarie entered a private Catholic school. Alma hoped to resume the volunteer work she had pursued at other bases. But she soon discovered that all volunteer work at Fort Carson was under the control of Ann Hudachek. This was frustrating, because it meant that anything one of the wives wanted to do had to be approved by Mrs. Hudachek. Despite being advised to not get involved, Powell decided to discuss the situation with General Hudachek, suggesting to him that other wives be allowed to participate more fully and freely in the volunteer activities. Hudachek said nothing in the course of the conversation, but called his wife after Powell left his office. The Powells soon found out that the Hudacheks were not happy with them. Alma was summoned for tea with Ann Hudachek, where her disapproval with Alma was expressed in no uncertain terms.

It was obvious that the Fourth Mechanized had serious morale problems, and in Powell's view, the cause was Hudachek's management style—which relied more on intimidation than it did on positive motivation. Still, Powell enjoyed being in the unit and assumed his relationship with Hudachek was basically sound. Which made the evaluation Powell received from Hudachek in the spring of 1982 all the more shocking. In effect, Hudachek gave Powell a lukewarm evaluation—a report that Powell understood immediately would end his career at the brigadier general rank. When the evaluation was endorsed by Hudachek's immediate superior, Powell was certain he would be leaving the Army shortly, since a mediocre evaluation meant that he would not be promoted. He was terribly disappointed, especially since his earlier evaluations had been so positive and were the basis for his advancement not only in the military but in government as well. After a few days, Powell decided not to be a crybaby but to accept reality as a mature adult. He assumed he would be job hunting as a civilian in a matter of months.

Much to his surprise, however, Powell received notification that he was going to be appointed the deputy commanding general of the Combined Arms Combat Development Activity (CACDA) in Fort Leavenworth, Kansas. This job was normally filled by a major general (two stars). Had his career been salvaged, and if so, by whom? Powell soon learned that General Richard G. Cavazos, the head of all U.S.-based army forces and the commander of Forces Command (FORSCOM) maintained a close watch on all his generals. He had seen Hudachek and Powell up close, and he understood that Hudachek was a difficult commander. Cavazos chose to ignore the lukewarm evaluation and moved Powell up to the CACDA operation. Shortly after assuming his new position, Powell learned he would be promoted to major general.

The return to Fort Leavenworth was a welcome change. Unlike their earlier stay, this time the Powells would be living in a beautiful large house. Alma at last could feel that they had graduated from the more humble examples of military housing. The job was interesting, and since he had survived the close call of the lukewarm evaluation, Powell could look forward to the opportunity to command a full division. But once again, a fateful telephone call from Washington intervened. This time, Caspar Weinberger wanted Powell to become his chief military assistant. It was the last thing he wanted, and Powell begged to be spared from this promotion. He even told Weinberger personally that he did not want to return to the Pentagon for this kind of job. That made Weinberger want him even more; the Secretary felt that any good military man would prefer to command men in the field rather than sit in a Washington office. After eleven short months at Fort Leavenworth, the Powells packed up and returned to Washington.

Working for Weinberger was a totally different experience from earlier Pentagon assistantships. A fastidious man, Weinberger lived by punctual routines. He arrived at his office every morning precisely at 7 A.M.—not 7:01 or 6:59. Exactly two minutes before his arrival, his driver would telephone Powell and alert him that the Secretary was two minutes from arrival. Weinberger sat behind an enormous desk that had once been used by General John Pershing, the commander of U.S. forces in Europe during World War I. A former lawyer and TV commentator, Weinberger played his cards close to his vest—he rarely showed emotion and was considered one of the most stubborn people in government. He also had a secret obsession for chocolate, and Powell soon found out that one of the drawers in the Pershing desk was filled with candy bars and Hershey's Kisses.

As Weinberger's military aide, Powell was responsible for controlling the Secretary's time and access to him. He also performed any other function that Weinberger chose to use him for. This was no job dealing with the requisition of spare parts or long-range theories about force requirements. The best part of the assignment was simply its location—at the highest level of government, where national and international issues were decided. Within a few weeks of his return, Powell was in the thick of the Korean Airlines Flight 007 disaster. The Soviet military had shot down a Korean commercial airliner that had drifted off course and over Soviet territory in the Far East while flying from Alaska to Seoul, South Korea. The shootdown had killed 269 people and created an international crisis, with the United States accusing the Soviets of intentionally murdering innocent travelers and the Soviets accusing the United States of using a commercial airplane to spy on their territory. The incident was typical of what happens during high-level crisis management—calls in the middle of the night, meetings at odd hours, dealing with the media. Powell learned a couple of important lessons. First, get all the details and don't make assumptions on partial information. Second, get information out to the media as soon as possible and not in dribs and drabs.

Weinberger, a correct and formal man who liked old-fashioned courtliness and ritual, was a master of public relations and knew how to anticipate problems that could arise with the media. Every morning, at 8:30 A.M., he held a staff meeting—a large gathering with many faces from many departments. Unlike his predecessor Harold Brown, who preferred small and short meetings, Weinberger enjoyed presiding over a large group of people who voiced different opinions. In the end, Weinberger made the decisions, but morale was high among his staff because people felt included. The big tent approach to meetings was something Powell agreed with and adopted.

In October 1983, shortly after assuming his job with Weinberger, the U.S. military suffered a disastrous loss when the marine barracks in Beirut, Lebanon, was bombed. President Reagan, on the advice of his national security adviser, Robert C. MacFarlane, had approved sending a contingent of marines to Beirut in order to serve as a buffer zone between warring Lebanese factions and the Israeli army, which had invaded Lebanon in 1982 in pursuit of Palestinian terrorists. It was exactly the kind of mission that Powell had come to distrust—undefined, vague, with no clear end, and most important of all, potentially deadly for the military personnel involved. When one faction of Lebanese extremists drove a truck bomb on a suicide mission directly into the building housing the Americans, 241 marines died. The United States had gotten involved in an age-old factional conflict. In doing so, it became a part of that conflict, not a neutral observer as had originally been intended. Powell became more determined than ever to oppose such use of U.S. military forces in the future.

Perhaps one of the most important experiences Powell got as Weinberger's military aide was to be the gatekeeper. He was required to consider the needs of the four service chiefs, the three service secretaries, and any other high-ranking Pentagon official whenever they wanted access to Weinberger. This balancing—listening to the points of view of head-strong people defending their turfs—was valuable Pentagon training for being Chairman of the Joint Chiefs of Staff.

It was Weinberger who introduced Powell personally to President Ronald Reagan. He had seen Reagan from afar, but one day, when he Weinberger went to the White House for a meeting with the president, the secretary brought Powell to Reagan. Powell was deeply impressed by the president, who was meticulously dressed and who projected a radiant optimism that impressed everyone who met him.

The year 1984 was personally difficult for Colin and Alma. On February 5, 1984, Alma's father died. That spring, Colin's mother entered the final stages of her illness. She was suffering from both a heart condition and cancer, and Colin tried as often as possible to come up to New York on weekends to be with her. Finally, on June 3, 1984, Maud Powell died, surrounded by her loving family. Her funeral service was held at the old St. Margaret's Church in the Bronx. For Powell, it was not only a time of grief but also of reflection on the blessings he had had as a child with such a loving and supportive family.

The assignment in Weinberger's office was supposed to last two years. When it was over, Powell was led to believe that he would be given command of the Eighth Infantry Division (Mechanized) in Germany. This was exactly what he had hoped for as a two-star general: command of a full division. But Weinberger did not want to give Powell up just yet. He intervened and told the disappointed Powell that after his extended stay at the Pentagon, he would be given a corps command, that is, command of two full divisions. A skeptical Powell had no choice but to accede to the Secretary's wishes. If he wanted to advance to a command, he would not do it by antagonizing the Secretary of Defense. Moreover, Powell had nothing but the highest respect for Weinberger and Reagan. He believed they had saved the morale of the military and restored the nation's confidence in its fighting forces. While acknowledging that Carter and Brown had planned many new military systems and modernizations, it was Weinberger and Reagan who had the willpower and political clout to make them happen.

Powell planned to stay with Weinberger until the spring of 1986. But in the months before his departure, a disturbing event began to unfold in government, one that would, in the years ahead, not only threaten Powell's career but also the very presidency of Ronald Reagan. In June 1985, a memo from National Security Adviser Robert MacFarlane to Weinberger passed across Powell's desk. In it was the outline of a plan to improve U.S. relations with Iran by selling the Iranian government American-made anti-tank missiles. Weinberger was appalled at the suggestion. It had been only four years since the Iranians had released the American hostages held from 1979 to 1981. Now here was a plan hatched in Mac-Farlane's National Security Council to sell this country sophisticated armaments! MacFarlane met with Weinberger and explained that the sale would encourage moderate elements within Iran. Weinberger remarked that the only moderates in Iran were in cemeteries, having all been executed by the radical regime. Powell also believed that the idea was idiotic. Both he and Weinberger hoped it would just go away.

To their surprise and disgust, however, they were to discover that the plan continued to be developed in secret, largely because the president was interested in it and would not close it down. Reagan hoped that this deal might lead to the freeing of U.S. hostages being held in Beirut, Lebanon, by Lebanese factions supported by the Iranians. Over the disapproval of Weinberger, Reagan ordered that more than 4,000 anti-tank missiles be transferred to Iran. They were to be moved from their warehouses in the military to the CIA, which would then forward them to Iran. Under the law, Congress was supposed to be notified whenever a major arms transfer to a foreign country occurred, but they were not. Weinberger and Powell were reluctant participants in the deal because they were required to coordinate with the CIA and make sure that the president's orders were carried out. Little did Powell realize at the time what a disaster this plan would later wreak on the American government.

In March 1986 Colin Powell was promoted to lieutenant general (three stars). To his delight, Weinberger lived up to his promise, giving Powell command of the V Corps in Germany. He would be returning to the place where he had begun his military career twenty-eight years earlier. But now, instead of the single gold bar of a second lieutenant on his shoulders, Powell carried the three stars of a lieutenant general. Instead of commanding a handful of men in a platoon, Powell had responsibility over 75,000 men gathered in the V Corps, which consisted of the Eighth Infantry Division and the Third Armored Division. Instead of living in the humble bachelor's quarters, he now occupied a spacious house on the outskirts of Frankfurt and had his own driver. Powell was nervous about the new job. It had been several years since his last real command, and he had skipped over commanding a full division to a corps command. The division commanders who reported to him were older than he was. Powell did not want to be considered a political general, a creature who came from the halls of the Pentagon and who was far removed from the realities of a field command.

Powell, of course, had much Pentagon experience. There was no way to deny that. But he was also an extraordinarily smart and sensitive commander. Before leaving for Germany, he and Alma took intensive German lessons. They were also required by the Pentagon to take a course in defensive driving that taught them how to escape a terrorist kidnapping. But most important, he took with him two principles he had learned years ago and continued to live by as a high-ranking military man: "Accomplish the mission and look after the troops."[2] He was always concerned about the well being of the troops. An army with a high morale is a better fighting force. And he knew that morale was rooted not only in such tangibles as good pay and housing, or a sense of promotion—which were vital—but also in a belief that the work the military people did mattered and was appreciated.

As a commander, Powell wanted his subordinates to be honest and not hide bad news from him. In his words, "Bad news isn't wine. It doesn't improve with age."[3] But once he had made a decision, Powell expected complete loyalty from his subordinates. The forces he commanded in 1986 were basically in the same position on the ground that they had been twenty-eight years earlier, when Powell began his first German tour in Gelnhausen: American might faced Soviet might across the Iron Curtain that ran down the middle of Germany. In 1986, however, the international atmosphere was alive with a hope for better U.S.-Soviet relations. In 1985, after a succession of old leaders who died after a short time in office, the Soviet Communist party selected Mikhail Gorbachev as its leader, and, therefore, the leader of the country. Gorbachev was in his mid-50s and wanted to bring reform to his nation's politics and prosperity for his people. Although major differences still existed between the United States and the Soviet Union, Gorbachev and Reagan had begun a dialogue to reduce tensions.

Perhaps this was one of the reasons Powell found the job far less stressful than his recent service in Washington had been. There were no phone calls in the middle of night; the workday ended at 5 P.M., at which time he would play a game of racquetball with his driver and head on home for dinner with Alma. One relaxing moment was a journey on a luxury train that had belonged to the German dictator Hitler during the Nazi period in Germany and was now available for use by U.S. officers. Powell invited an old friend, Ron Lauder, the U.S. ambassador to Austria, and his wife for a trip from Frankfurt to Berlin. Also contributing to Powell's contentment with his new post was the fact that his son Mike, a second lieutenant, was stationed with the VII Corps, also in Germany. Although they didn't have many opportunities to visit each other, they kept in touch by letter. Powell was delighted that Mike, on his own and without parental advice, had decided to make a career in the military, even though he had turned down an appointment to West Point.

But in Washington, the Reagan administration was about to face its greatest crisis—one that threatened to bring down Reagan himself. On November 1, 1986, an Arab-language magazine in Beirut, Lebanon, published a story revealing that the United States had sold arms to Iran. That part alone was sensational enough, but a few days later, another sensational aspect of the story was about to break in the newspapers. Before it did, the administration decided to go public to avoid excessive embarrassment. Attorney General Edwin Meese announced that the price of the missiles had been jacked up before the sale to the Iranians in order to create profits, which were then diverted into a secret bank account. This money was then given to the Contras, a group of rebels fighting the Communist-friendly Nicaraguan government in Central America. Congress had passed a law prohibiting any U.S. assistance to the Contras. The secret bank account with the profits from the Iran arms sales was a way of getting around the law.

What was distressing to Powell was that this operation had been run from within the White House, under the direction of the current national security adviser, Admiral John Poindexter, and his aide, Lieutenant Colonel Oliver North. The president and secretary of defense apparently knew nothing about the diversion of the money to the Contras, which in itself was a disaster. Why didn't the president know about the activities of some of his closest aides? Poindexter resigned and North was fired by Reagan. The National Security Council was in disarray. Rumors were circulating that Frank Carlucci would be named to replace Poindexter. Powell thought that was a superb choice, but when the phone rang and Powell learned that Carlucci was on the line, his heart sank.

NOTES

1. Powell, *My American Journey*, p. 197.
2. Ibid., p. 308.
3. Ibid., p. 309.

Chapter 7

NATIONAL SECURITY COUNCIL: ADVISER TO THE PRESIDENT

"Colin, you've got to come back," were Frank Carlucci's first words to Powell.[1] The very thought made Powell queasy. He had been commanding the V Corps for barely five months, and once again he was being snatched away from what he wanted most and thrust back into the political mess in Washington. The Iran-Contra scandal was something he had not caused, but he was indirectly involved in it. He warned Carlucci that he could be tainted because he had helped in the transfer of the anti-tank missiles from the military to the CIA. Carlucci checked it out with the legal staff and came back and told Powell he was not in trouble.

What Carlucci wanted was for Powell to serve as the deputy national security adviser to the President. Powell resisted, but Carlucci said he would call again and hoped Powell would reconsider. But the next person to call was Weinberger. Powell still resisted, even though both Weinberger and Carlucci pointed out that Powell's unique skills at organization and at bringing order out of chaos were what was needed at this moment of peril for the president. Powell reminded them that after only five months in Germany, he would suffer irreparable damage to his career as a commander if he left so early in his tour. Powell had been told earlier that he would have an unconventional career. Now, a friend told him bluntly that he was not destined to be a commander. He was wanted in Washington. Powell did not want to hear these words.

Then, on December 12, 1986, the phone at home rang. Alma answered. It was Ronald Reagan, and he wanted to speak with Colin. Reagan's tone was friendly and informal; he told Powell that he needed him and that he hoped he would join the team in the White House during these troubled times. Powell—always the military man—could not refuse his commander in chief. He would be going back to Washington, to a job where he again would be out of uniform. For Alma, it meant trekking back to the United States, and for his youngest, Annemarie, it meant returning to the high school she had left just five months before.

On January 2, 1987, Powell reported for work in the West Wing of the White House. His new office was the same size as his bathroom at V Corps in Germany. Powell had barely sat down when a tall, thin man entered his office to welcome him and introduce himself. It was George Bush, vice president of the United States, and he and Powell would be sharing a bathroom in the West Wing. Such was the first meeting between two men whose careers would be forever linked in the years ahead.

The National Security Council that Carlucci and Powell inherited was in a state of collapse. Something needed to be done quickly to restore its operations and its credibility. Under MacFarlane and Poindexter, it had gotten involved in areas that were none of its business. One of the first things Carlucci and Powell did was to announce that the NSC would not be involved in secret operations overseas. That was the territory of the CIA. The NSC's original mission was to serve as a clearinghouse for the recommendations that arose in the various departments of government affecting national security. The National Security Adviser was supposed to synthesize recommendations from all the relevant departments and then make recommendations of his own to the president. The NSC was not intended to be a freelance operation that went off on its own with diplomatic, military, and covert operations. Some of its previous ventures bordered on the unbelievable. In their efforts to cultivate Iranian moderates, MacFarlane and North had arrived in Teheran on a secret trip bearing a cake and Bibles as gifts for the Iranian leadership—the same violently anti-American, anti-Western Islamic leadership that had executed thousands of its political enemies and brutalized American hostages just a few years before.

But as Powell soon discovered, a renegade NSC was possible only in a White House in which Ronald Reagan was president. In their almost daily meetings with Reagan, Carlucci and Powell observed that the president was often very detached from his job. Reagan listened intently but would rarely express an opinion. When Powell or Carlucci expressed a preference, Reagan would often chime in and agree. Carlucci often wondered out loud what had been decided at meetings. He instructed Powell to keep careful notes on all their meetings with Reagan. What Powell came to understand was that in a White House in which the president was often uninvolved, individuals were free to go off on their own and pursue their own projects. According to Poindexter and North, Reagan had been told about the Iranian arms policy in detail. But Reagan remembered things differently, and years later refused to concede that the purpose of the arms sales was to try to get the hostages in Lebanon released. In 1987, Reagan was 76 years old; he had suffered a gunshot wound six years before and surgery for colon cancer in 1985. Although he looked good for his age and was always cheerful and optimistic, he was slowing down both mentally and physically. With a management style that was always detached, even as a younger man, Reagan was perhaps as much a victim of his age as he was of anything.

In order to structure and focus the recommendations of the NSC for Reagan, Powell and Carlucci created the Policy Review Group (PRG), an interagency body within the NSC made up of outstanding officials who gathered to make and coordinate policy recommendations. Powell conducted the meetings, and his goal was to create clearly stated policy that everyone understood and agreed on. Policies that had been created with the input of all relevant departments could then be summarized for Reagan for information or decision. This was one way to prevent individuals so inclined from going off on their own paths with their pet projects.

As far as the Contras were concerned, Powell quickly came to the conclusion that they were weaker and less effective than anyone had wanted to believe. The Contras represented an honorable objective—to rid Nicaragua of a Marxist regime whose policies were impoverishing an already poor country. But they were a rag-tag army, and Congress had consistently refused to give them arms. The law had to be obeyed. Powell worked to get humanitarian aid from Congress, but legally obtained armaments remained out of reach.

In response to the outcry over the Iran-Contra affair, President Reagan appointed an independent commission headed by Senator John Tower of Texas to investigate the scandal. The Tower Commission's report, issued in February 1987, was critical of Reagan's lax management style and of Weinberger for not having worked harder to find out what the NSC was up to. Powell felt the report was unfair to Weinberger. But the worst was yet to come. In the spring of 1987, Congress began public hearings on Iran-Contra. For the first time, the public got an insight into Reagan's White House and some of its less admirable characters. Oliver North, in particular, came across as a somewhat dangerous personality, who, although clearly a patriot, had a tendency to go off on his own in spectacular and unpredictable ways. Paper-shredding, cloak-and-dagger operations, and documents being smuggled out of the West Wing in the pantyhose of North's secretary were not the kinds of stories that inspired confidence in the

American people. Luckily for Reagan and the country, Carlucci and Powell quickly restored the reputation and a sense of balance to the NSC.

Powell had barely settled into his new job when he received word that his son Mike had been severely injured in an automobile accident in Germany. Shortly after receiving the bad news, Powell and Alma hitched a ride on a cargo plane, arriving in Germany the following morning. Mike was transferred to Walter Reed Army Medical Center in Washington in a matter of days, but he faced surgeries and a long recovery before he could walk again and resume normal activity. The accident was a shock to Colin and Alma and made them realize how lucky they had been not to lose Mike.

In the fall of 1987, Caspar Weinberger announced his intention to resign as Secretary of Defense. He had been on the job for almost seven years. Of late, Congress had been giving him more and more trouble over his budget requests. In addition, he believed that he was losing influence with the president. The First Lady, Nancy Reagan, had never been a great fan of Weinberger's, and now she believed he represented an overly aggressive, military approach toward the Soviet Union. Mrs. Reagan wanted the president to be remembered as a peacemaker and encouraged him to pursue better relations with Gorbachev's Soviet Union. Weinberger understood that loss of confidence on the part of the first lady meant it was time to go. In any event, his wife was ailing and he was in his early 70s, so retirement seemed appropriate.

As his replacement, Reagan promoted Frank Carlucci from head of the National Security Council to Secretary of Defense. Powell thought this might be a good time to return to the army. Predictably, however, it was not to be. Howard Baker, the White House Chief of Staff, called on Powell and told him the news—Reagan wanted Powell to be the new National Security Adviser. The young army officer who had reluctantly interviewed with the NSC head just ten years before was now about to become the head of the very organization itself. The job required approval by the Senate. It had cabinet-level status and meant that Powell would be in the news every day. Realizing that the Reagan administration had only a year left in office, Powell felt it was important to help maintain stability in foreign affairs, especially given the high turnover in the NSC. So he accepted the job, once again yearning for the day when he might return to a command position in his beloved army.

Within a month after taking over, Powell and Secretary of State George P. Shultz were off to Geneva, Switzerland, to work out the final details on a treaty with the Soviet Union reducing each nation's intermediate nuclear forces (INF). Intermediate nuclear weapons did not have the long range of intercontinental ballistic missiles (ICBMs), which were the most powerful nuclear weapons targeted on the enemy's cities thousands of miles away. Nor were they as small as tactical nuclear weapons, which were intended to be used on the battlefield, for example, if there were a ground war in Europe. But the reduction of INF weapons represented a major de-escalation of the arms competition between the United States and the USSR.

On his return from Geneva, Powell flew to California to brief the president at his ranch in the mountains near Santa Barbara. Both the president and first lady (who did not officially attend the briefing but hovered nearby arranging flowers and listening to what was being discussed) were delighted with the outcome. Within a short time, Gorbachev would be coming to Washington for a ceremonial visit to initial the treaty. The visit to commemorate the INF treaty was a symbolic occasion that revealed something about President Reagan—a reality that Powell clearly understood. For all his problems as a poor manager, and despite the criticism of him because of the military build-up of the early 1980s, Reagan was genuinely interested in helping create a more peaceful world free from the threat of nuclear destruction.

The Gorbachev visit was the first taste Powell had of a summit meeting that he was partially responsible for conducting. Even before Gorbachev set foot on American soil, there was a problem. Mrs. Reagan had invited Gorbachev's wife, Raisa, for tea or a dinner—her choice. There was no response from the Soviets, and Mrs. Reagan was getting angry. Powell pressured the Soviet ambassador in Washington to get an answer to the invitation. Finally, the invitation to tea was accepted and a crisis between the two first ladies, who clearly did not like each other, was averted—at least for the time being.

Gorbachev arrived on December 7. Powell's first impression of him was that he was quick-witted, intelligent, and totally in command of the facts and figures pertaining to nuclear issues. At his first meeting with Reagan, a large gathering was held in the cabinet room of the White House; Gorbachev spoke first. The Soviet leader was adamantly opposed to the American construction of a nuclear shield in space called the Strategic Defense Initiative (SDI), popularly known in the press as "Star Wars." In Reagan's eyes, SDI was purely defensive. It was meant to shoot down ICBMs fired at the United States while they were still in space. For Gorbachev, however, they were a one-sided weapons system that gave almost all the power to the United States. Before Gorbachev finished his talk, Reagan interrupted him and told a corny joke that no one laughed at—not even the Americans. Gorbachev paused for a moment, pretended nothing had been said, then continued with his presentation, and Reagan followed with a few generalities before the group adjourned. The meeting showed how ill-prepared Reagan was and was embarrassing to Powell and the American delegation.

Powell felt partially responsible for the president's poor performance and was determined to prepare him before the next meeting that was scheduled for the following day. That evening, while the Reagans entertained the Gorbachevs at a state dinner in the White House, Powell and his staff labored into the night to produce detailed briefing notes on cards for Reagan to use the next morning. Before the meeting, Powell sat down with Reagan and reviewed the talking points. Reagan was always at his best when he had talking points on cards, typed, double-spaced, and organized in a logical way. A former movie actor, he was superb when he played the part from a written script; Powell was quick to realize that he needed to keep it simple and insisted that the president speak first.

Not surprisingly, Reagan was at his best, and the unpleasant impression of the day before was erased in a good final meeting with Gorbachev. The next objective was to get a treaty on ICBMs. The so-called START talks (strategic arms limitation talks) to limit the big missiles could not begin until both sides agreed to a goal on the total number of long-range missiles each side would be allowed to have. The Russians wanted a ceiling of 5,100, but the Americans wanted 4,800. As Gorbachev got ready to leave the White House for Moscow, Powell, Carlucci, and the Soviets huddled in the cabinet room trying to arrive at compromise. Carlucci suggested 4,900, which the Soviets accepted. Reagan agreed, and the START talks were put on track as Gorbachev departed for home.

In the course of his first months as National Security Adviser, Powell did a great deal of traveling with Secretary of State George Shultz. He came to respect the secretary for his intelligence and good judgment. Shultz had served in government since the Nixon administration. He deeply respected Ronald Reagan and believed that one of his jobs was to give substance to Reagan's vision of America's place in the world. Powell also came to respect Anatoly Dobrynin, the long-time Soviet ambassador to the United States. Dobrynin, a thoughtful man well-schooled in the politics of Washington and Moscow, told Powell that Gorbachev was interested in making fundamental changes to the Soviet system, changes that would better the lives of the average Soviet citizen. Dobrynin, of course, was talking about changing the existing system and had no way of knowing that the entire Soviet system would collapse in two short years. But the Soviet ambassador did reinforce Powell's impression of Gorbachev as a leader with amazing vision and intelligence.

Another thing Powell learned through firsthand experience was how to deal with the Washington media. As national security adviser, he was required to give interviews and press conferences on an almost daily basis. He learned the hard way that a slip of the tongue could cause major problems. On one occasion, he expressed a point of view that, unknown to him at the time, seemed to be in opposition to something the president had said just minutes before. The resulting hysteria on the part of the White House press office was a lesson. You can't control what questions are asked, but you can control which ones are answered. And not every question needs to be answered. At the White House, everyone, especially the National Security Adviser, needs to be in agreement about what is said to the media. If one official says one thing, and another appears to contradict, the public will be left with the impression that the administration is not consistent and has no officially stated policy—a situation that could be very dangerous in foreign affairs.

One of the most important foreign trips during 1988 was President Reagan's visit to the Soviet Union, which began in late May. Some 800 people—government officials, press, and others—accompanied the president to Moscow. Reagan had about seven months left in office, so in many ways the visit represented the culmination of his foreign policy, especially his efforts to normalize relations with the Soviet Union. The INF treaty was due to be ratified by the Senate a few days before the departure for the Soviet Union. In the weeks preceding the trip, Powell was enlisted to help convince conservative members of the Senate that the treaty was beneficial to the United States and that Gorbachev was genuinely interested in reform and better relations. Many U.S. officials were having a difficult time adjusting to the new realities, especially after forty years of hostility between the two superpowers. On May 28, the day before the president's arrival in Moscow, the Senate ratified the treaty.

At his best, Reagan was a masterful performer in public situations. The media highlight of the trip was his stroll through Red Square with Gorbachev, meeting and shaking hands with ordinary Russians and fielding impromptu questions from the press. Overall, the meeting was a success. But as the U.S. party prepared to depart, Gorbachev suggested issuing a joint statement in which each side pledged not to interfere with the political systems in the other's sphere of influence. At first, Powell saw nothing wrong with the statement, but more experienced officials in the State Department pointed out that the real point of the communiqué was to get the United States to endorse such existing realities as the Soviet domination of Lithuania, Latvia, and Estonia—formerly independent nations that were absorbed by the Soviet Union in the early 1940s.

On the advice of his advisers, Reagan refused to support this particular communiqué. With just minutes to go before the Americans' departure, Gorbachev continued to push aggressively for the statement. At that point, Powell intervened and told Gorbachev politely but forcefully that the United States could not and would not issue this joint communiqué. His language was polite but blunt. Gorbachev simply shrugged his shoulders and said okay. The dispute ended and the Reagans and their party left for Washington. It was an important moment for Powell, because for the first time he publicly stepped out of his role as a behind-the-scenes manager.

That summer, Powell became involved in a dispute between the army and the navy over who should be appointed to a major command. The command in question was known as CENTCOM—Central Command—which was responsible for U.S. forces in the Middle East and Southwest Asia. Because many Muslim countries in the region did not want an American command headquartered in their countries, CENTCOM's command post was at MacDill Air Force Base in Florida. Since the retiring commander was a navy man, the army felt the new commander should be from its ranks. The Chairman of the Joint Chiefs of Staff, Admiral Crowe, recommended a navy officer, but the final decision was in the hands of Defense Secretary Carlucci. Powell believed that an army man would be the better choice, since CENTCOM's mission was to serve as a ground force in the desert—not a naval force. Carlucci agreed, and appointed General H. Norman Schwarzkopf of the U.S. Army as commander of CENTCOM. Powell and Schwarzkopf would be partners on the world stage just a few short years ahead.

In November 1988, Vice President George Bush was elected 41st President of the United States. Powell and Bush had disagreed in 1988 over an issue in Central American policy, and at the time Bush had expressed his displeasure with Powell. Nevertheless, Bush wanted Powell to be a part of his administration; Powell in turn respected Bush as a man of unquestioned integrity. After his election, Bush told Powell that he wanted his own man—Brent Scowcroft—as national security adviser. He suggested to Powell that Deputy Secretary of State was a possibility, or perhaps head of the Central Intelligence Agency (CIA). Powell felt the first position would be a demotion, and the second was beyond his abilities or interest. He wanted to return to the army, and he told Bush, who graciously accepted his decision. The position he was slated for was commander of

Forces Command (FORSCOM), the head of all U.S. Army forces in the United States. It was a command over more than 1 million people.

On his last day at the NSC, January 20, 1989, Powell paid a farewell visit to his office in the West Wing of the White House. His belongings had already been removed and the office painted in anticipation of Brent Scowcroft's arrival. At noon, George Bush was sworn in as president. Powell looked forward to what he assumed would be his final command before his retirement.

NOTE

1. Powell, *My American Journey*, p. 318.

Secretary of State Colin Powell and his wife Alma Powell deplane in Budapest, Hungary, May 28, 2001. Powell arrived in the Hungarian capital from his four-nation African tour to attend meetings of NATO ministers. (AP Photo.)

As Chairman of the Joint Chiefs of Staff, Colin Powell visited U.S. troops in Saudi Arabia in September 1990. Here he surveys a Marine position near the border with Kuwait as Marine Corporal Vincent Rivero stands guard. (AP Photo.)

Secretary of Defense Caspar Weinberger meets with Colin Powell and Captain James P. Cormack at the Pentagon, 1983. (Defense Visual Information Center.)

General Colin Powell, Chairman of the Joint Chiefs of Staff, General Norman Schwarzkopf, commander, U.S. Central Command, and Mrs. Schwarzkopf ride in the welcome home parade honoring the men and women who served in Desert Storm, June 10, 1991. (Defense Visual Information Center.)

Chapter 8

THE HIGHEST COMMAND: LEADING THE MILITARY IN PEACE AND WAR

As Colin Powell assumed command of FORSCOM, he had every reason to believe that he had reached the highest position he would ever hold in the U.S. Army. He was 52 years old, and with the FORSCOM command came his fourth star. He was now a full general; the highest rank the army offered in peacetime. From his vantage point as the commander of all army forces in the United States, Powell believed he would continue to work toward his goal to bring the army—or at least the portion of it he controlled—into the modern world. His service as national security adviser had given him an inside view of the Soviet Union and international relations. Gorbachev, to Powell, was indeed a reformer. But from Powell's point of view, the Cold War had already been won by the United States. Gorbachev wanted to reform the Soviet communist system. Powell believed that it was not reformable, and that some day, in some way no one could predict, the entire Soviet system would be replaced.

For the time being, however, it was clear that the Soviets were no longer the ominous threat they had been in the years following World War II. By 1989, Gorbachev had drastically cut the size of the Soviet military by more than half a million men. He had entered into an arms reduction treaty with the United States and was discussing further reductions. And, most important, he had withdrawn Soviet forces from neighboring Afghanistan, where they had been following a Soviet invasion more than a decade before. The pullout from Afghanistan was the Soviet equivalent of the U.S. loss in Vietnam. The Soviets were saying, in effect, that they were no longer able to intervene in other countries, even small, powerless ones on their border. The Soviets were too poor. They could not afford the upkeep of a large military force; they could barely feed their own people.

The problem with the U.S. military, in Powell's mind, was that its leaders were far too slow to recognize this change. As a result, they still wanted to fight the old war in the old ways. The army needed new strategies and a new mission, and moving its leaders in that direction was no small objective. Powell saw an army of the future that had the ability to field small mobile forces wherever needed. Flexibility, rather than massive retaliation, would be needed to meet post–Cold War challenges.

The pace of the new job at FORSCOM was a welcome change from the NSC. There was a comfortable house on the grounds of Fort McPherson, Georgia, where FORSCOM was headquartered. At the NSC, Powell had to drive himself to work every morning in his own not-so-new car. At FORSCOM, he was entitled to a driver to take him to and from work. It seemed like a comfortable way to wind up a distinguished military career.

In August of 1989, Powell attended a meeting of army general officers in Baltimore. It was an informal gathering at a conference center outside of the city, and it gave this unique fraternity of brother officers a chance to exchange ideas and get to know one other. In this relaxed setting, Powell received a message that Secretary of Defense Dick Cheney wanted to see him immediately at the Pentagon. Cheney, a former congressman from Wyoming, had been the White House Chief of Staff in the administration of President Gerald R. Ford in the mid-1970s. He had not been President Bush's first choice for the Pentagon job, but after his first nomination—John Tower, author of the Tower Commission report—was all but rejected by the Senate, Cheney was chosen. Powell considered Cheney to be brilliant and tough as nails. He had visited Powell at FORSCOM headquarters just a few months before.

Powell knew what the meeting was likely to be about, but he dared not think too much about it. The current Chairman of the Joint Chiefs of Staff, Admiral Crowe, was retiring after four years on the job. There were always numerous candidates for the job of chairman, and it was customary to rotate the position among the services. Since a navy man currently held the job, another service would now fill the position. Powell arrived at the Pentagon clad in slacks and loafers, so sudden had the summons to Washington been. He was taken into Cheney's office, where the secretary wasted no time in letting him know the purpose of the meeting. Cheney wanted Powell to be the new Chairman of the JCS. Powell, of course, was flattered and overwhelmed. There were fifteen generals who were senior to him in line for the job. Indeed, he had received his fourth star only a few months before. Cheney said that the final choice, of course, was up to

President Bush, but that if Powell agreed, Cheney would recommend him for the job. According to Cheney, the only reservation Bush had was that Powell was a junior general. Would the other generals resent him and make his job difficult? Powell felt they would not. He knew them and believed they would wish him well. Cheney and Bush wanted Powell because of his broad experience not only as a commander but also as someone experienced in national security issues and in diplomacy. Powell replied that if the President wanted him, he would serve. And thus, the ROTC cadet from the Bronx, the son of poor Jamaican immigrants, ascended to the highest position in the U.S. military. It was more than an American dream—it was an American dream come true.

The Joint Chiefs of Staff (JCS) was established in the early 1940s, at the beginning of the U.S. entry into World War II. It was a kind of committee made up of the leaders (the chiefs of staff) of branches of the military. Before then, there had been no overriding body that coordinated the different branches of the military in combined operations. After the war, Congress made the JCS a permanent body. By the end of the twentieth century, the JCS consisted of the heads of the army, navy, air force, and marines, plus the chairman, who was selected by the president and had to be ratified by the Senate.

Although the idea behind the JCS was to coordinate policy recommendations to the president, the system had serious drawbacks, which Powell, as a student of military affairs, was well aware of. One of the functions of the Joint Chiefs of Staff was to give advice to the president. Each member, however, had a potential built-in conflict: he had to represent the interests of *his* branch of the service, yet he was supposed to act on the committee to represent the good of the military and the nation as a whole. For example, the army chief of staff would want to keep the army strong with the latest weapons and fully staffed. However, there might be situations in that the army would be reduced in size for reasons having to do with the nation's overall defense needs. As a result of this tension, the reports that came out of the JCS were often watered down and uncontroversial, the result of the innumerable compromises needed to get everyone to agree on a policy recommendation. Under Admiral Crowe, the system was changed. In 1986, Congress passed legislation making the Chairman of the JCS the principle military adviser to the president. He would now be permitted to give his own advice to the president and was no longer required only to present the views of the other chiefs. Under the new law, the chiefs were also allowed to disagree publicly with the chairman. This new law allowed the president to receive a spectrum of views, not necessarily some watered-down memo that took months to create.

On October 3, 1989, the Powell family gathered at the Pentagon for a ceremony to welcome Powell as the new chairman of the Joint Chiefs. It was a momentous occasion for Alma, the children, Powell's sister and brother-in-law, and numerous aunts and uncles. Not only was he the youngest chairman in history, but he was the first African American. The formal ceremony continued in a joyous family gathering that went on late into the night.

In his first weeks as chairman, Powell gave much thought to the kind of a military that would be needed in the new world in which the Soviet Union was no longer the threat it had once been. Probably a smaller one, since the United States would no longer be facing down the Russian giant. Military thinkers had been used to imagining World War III in Europe, the massive Red Army sweeping across Germany into France. U.S. nuclear weapons, pointed at the Soviet Union, would be used to stop the Soviet forces if they invaded the West. This scenario was now a dead issue. It was not going to happen this way. But all of American strategic thinking, all weapons systems, all personnel levels and battlefield tactics were predicated on this kind of war. Powell knew that he had to start the process of educating the generals to think differently. And this was no small task. His service chiefs were not happy when he spoke of a smaller military. President Bush, a strategic thinker who understood Powell's point of view, had to think of political considerations and the need to bring Congress along in any large-scale reform. This also would not be easy, especially coming after a decade of unprecedented military expansion under President Reagan.

Powell's specific ideas had crystallized about the time he and Cheney were scheduled to appear before Congress to testify about the president's defense budget for the fiscal year 1991–1992. Powell had circulated his ideas for a "Base Force"—the terminology he applied to his reforms—among certain officials in the Pentagon and with a few influential members of Congress. After World War II, the United States military could have been described as a threat-based force. Its mission was to respond to the threat of the Soviet Union. In the New World, the U.S. military still needed to be able to respond to any and all kinds of threats; but in Powell's view, it now needed to be a threat- and capability-based force. The capability to perform differently defined missions needed to be added to our traditional abilities to respond to threats.

Powell saw the new military as having four basic missions: (1) the capability of fighting across the Atlantic Ocean; (2) of fighting across the Pacific; (3) the maintenance of a force at home capable of being deployed to hot spots around the world; and (4) maintenance of a nuclear force (now smaller than before because of the reduced threat from the Soviets and because of treaties with them reducing our nuclear stockpiles). These focused objectives would be reached with a smaller force. How much smaller would be the object of debate and of decision by the president and Congress. The 1991–1992 budget called for a reduction in military spending of some 2 percent. Over the long run, however, Powell believed that the military could be cut by 20 to 25 percent. In an unguarded moment, however, he mentioned this figure to a reporter who had been badgering him to be specific about the Base Force. When the story was published, a small firestorm broke out in the White House. Cheney was angry and asked Powell if he was a team player. Powell apologized and assured the defense secretary and the president that he was fully supportive of their decisions. By August of 1990, President Bush had signed on to the specifics of the Base Force reform.

Under Powell, the day-to-day operation of the office of the chairman changed dramatically, reflecting the changes Congress had voted on in 1986. Since Powell was no longer bound to reflect the consensus views of the chiefs, he felt that certain changes were necessary to reflect this reality. For one, he moved meetings with the chiefs into his personal office, a more intimate setting than the conference room they had previously been held in. He also had no published agendas for each meeting. The staffs of each of the chiefs were upset by this change because it threw the meetings open to any subject and did not give the chiefs a chance to prepare *their* agendas. Instead, Powell just went around the room and asked each chief to bring up any subject he felt needed to be aired. Powell, as the chief of the JCS, would bring up his subjects as well. Powell truly believed that this format would give the chiefs even more influence, since they could now spontaneously discuss their points of view without referring to some pre-digested memo prepared by their staff. Another important change: since Powell was no longer required to represent the chiefs' points of view to the president (although he frequently did), he saw no need to have formal votes on policy decisions. From Powell's point of view, this lack of formal voting was a positive development for the chiefs, because they could now claim that they had not voted for any unpopular decision by the chairman.

Powell preferred the light touch when dealing with subordinates. He expected people to work hard and to be loyal, but he was not a believer in driving people unfairly. When he was concentrating on a problem and was pressed for time, he did not want to be interrupted. If he was, he would sometimes lose his temper, but his outbursts were over quickly, and he urged his staff not to take them personally. Minor as some of these changes in the running of the JCS may have seemed at the time, they reflected the new reality that as chairman, Powell was a much more powerful and potentially influential figure in the president's council than any of his predecessors had ever been.

The reform and modernization of the military took place against a backdrop of real day-to-day affairs that took up Powell's time from the moment he woke up until late in the evening. So much of Powell's career as a soldier and national security adviser had been spent dealing with U.S.-Soviet relations. In his early weeks as chairman of the JCS, however, he faced a growing crisis in the Western Hemisphere—in the Central American nation of Panama.

Panama's history as an independent state was bound up with the United States. A province of the South American country of Colombia, it revolted and seceded from that nation in 1903—in an uprising supported by the United States. What the Americans wanted from Panama—and the reason they supported the secession from Colombia—was the right to build a canal across Panama linking the Atlantic with the Pacific Oceans. Such a canal would allow the U.S. Navy to move its ships from the Atlantic to the Pacific without having to sail all the way around the tip of South America. The canal and the strip of land surrounding it (the Panama Canal Zone) became a U.S. territory under the terms of a treaty that remained in effect until 1999, at which time the United States turned the canal and the Canal Zone over to the Panamanian government.

Throughout the twentieth century, America and Panama had a relationship that was at times stormy. Panamanian politics were unstable and rarely democratic. Even though there were elected leaders in the country, real power rested with the armed forces, the Panama Defense Force (PDF). The PDF would frequently overthrow the elected government, and the leader of the PDF was usually the strongman in Panama. The United States' sole concern was the security of the canal. If Panamanian politics—no matter how ugly or undemocratic—did not threaten the canal, the United States looked the other way.

By the late 1980s, however, Panama entered a period of extreme political instability. At the head of the PDF was a brutal and unpredictable dictator named Manuel Noriega. The U.S. government had supported many dictators throughout Latin America, but Noriega was different. He went too far. Although he received American money from the CIA, he was not a reliable client. In the 1980s, the United States government began to mount a campaign against the use of drugs. One aspect of this policy was to discourage the importation of drugs from foreign countries, especially Colombia. Noriega allowed Colombian drugs to be shipped to the United States through Panama and took vast amounts of money from drug dealers. To make it look like he was fighting drugs, Noriega occasionally staged phony arrests of drug dealers in Panama to ward off U.S. criticism. Noriega also tried to stay on the good side of some U.S. officials by supporting the illegal American Contra operation against the Marxist government of Nicaragua.

By the late 1980s, however, the U.S. government had had enough of Noriega, especially after he had a political opponent murdered. In 1988, a grand jury in Florida indicted Noriega for drug dealing. The U.S. government had to drop Noriega. But there were disagreements about what to do next. Secretary of State Shultz believed that force should be used to overthrow Noriega. Defense Secretary Carlucci believed that Noriega was only the tip of the iceberg. The real problem was the PDF, and that if Noriega were ousted, he would simply be replaced by another dictator coming out of the PDF organization.

The situation was unresolved when George Bush became President in January 1989. In May of that year, Noriega canceled a presidential election in which the polls showed a political opponent, Guillermo Endara, winning. Then, in front of American TV news cameras, he had another political opponent beaten up in the street. When a fellow PDF officer made an unsuccessful attempt to oust Noriega (an action in which the United States did not involve itself), Noriega had the man executed. By the time Powell came to the JCS, the belief in the use of force to oust Noriega was gaining ground in the Bush administration.

Powell was a great believer in restraint when it came to the use of the military. But in December 1989, an American marine stationed in Panama was shot and killed by PDF forces when he was off duty in Panama City, where he and a group of fellow Marines had gone in civilian clothes to have dinner. It was now clear that the lives of U.S. citizens and military personnel in Panama were in danger, and under these circumstances, Powell and Defense Secretary Cheney recommended immediate U.S. intervention to President Bush.

The action was named Operation Just Cause, and it would involve 13,000 American troops already stationed in the Canal Zone plus an additional 10,000 from the States, who would fly down on the first day of the invasion. Before President Bush approved, however, a meeting was held at the White House. Powell presented the military plan to the presi-

dent using charts and tables prepared by his assistants. The details had
been worked out by the commander in chief of the Southern Command
(SOUTHCOM), General Max Thurman, and by Lieutenant General
Carl Stiner, the commander of the XVIII Airborne Corps, which would
be providing the bulk of the troops being flown in from the United States.
Powell explained to the president that the main military objective was
the removal of Noriega *and* the PDF. The political goal was the installa-
tion of Guillermo Endara, the man who had really won the election, as
president of Panama.

Powell, all of the service chiefs, and Cheney were behind Just Cause, as
was the new Secretary of State, James Baker. National Security Adviser
Brent Scowcroft played a devil's advocate role: he wanted to know if we
had sufficient provocation to act. Powell said we did. He also wanted to
know how many casualties the United States would suffer. Powell said
there was no sure way of knowing, although he had told Cheney privately
that he expected around 20 American soldiers would be killed. Another
difficult question concerned the fate of Noriega: if we failed to capture
him, would the mission be considered a failure?

Bush's style as a leader was to sit quietly while his advisers argued among
themselves. He would ask an occasional question. Like Scowcroft, he was
also concerned about the number of casualties. As the commander in chief,
and as a veteran of combat in World War II, Bush was all too aware that the
fate of hundreds, even thousands, of young Americans rested ultimately in
his hands as president. Bush was also concerned that if Noriega escaped into
the jungle, Operation Just Cause would be portrayed in the media as only
partially successful. Powell could not answer how the failure to capture Noriega would play in the media or Congress, but he was candid in explaining
that there were no guarantees that Noriega could be captured immediately.
American intelligence—personal as well as electronic—had found him
very difficult to track on a daily basis. And the minute he became aware
that American troops were at the gates, he would be off running.

After several hours of discussion, Bush stood up and said, "Let's do it."
He had absorbed all the information he needed and had no difficulty at all
in making what he believed was the correct decision. Still, Powell worried
about Operation Just Cause. Any military operation consists of millions of
details that must all come together if it is to be a success. In Operation Just
Cause, thousands of troops were being shipped from the United States to
Panama, and their arrival had to be coordinated with the planned action
on the ground. It was winter in the States, and bad weather might cause
delays at the air bases that could hurt the campaign. And what were to be
the rules of engagement, that is, when could American firepower be used

and under what circumstances? Should U.S. fighters drop bombs on Noriega's villas, or would such attacks kill only servants and children? What would happen if firefights erupted on the narrow streets of Panama City? Although there were no clear answers to many of these questions, these and countless other details needed to be worked out.

President Bush also wanted Guillermo Endara, the opposition leader, to be sworn in as president before the military operation began. He wanted a government in place in Panama before the military action started. However, if Endara refused, for whatever reason, the operation would not proceed unless President Bush approved. On the evening of December 19, 1989, the day before the action was to begin, Cheney called Powell and told him that Endara had agreed to the U.S. plan. He would be taken to a U.S. Army facility and sworn in and thus be ready to assume control of the government the minute Noriega and the PDF had been neutralized.

Shortly before midnight, Powell joined Cheney and other military officials at the National Military Command Center in the Pentagon. This site was the nerve center of military operations. Filled with all kinds of sophisticated electronic equipment, the Command Center allowed leaders in Washington to be in touch with the action as it occurred. At 12:45 A.M., December 20, General Stiner, in Panama, gave the orders for the 193rd Infantry Brigade to leave the Canal Zone and attack Noriega's headquarters in Panama City. At the same time, F-117A fighter jets attacked the PDF headquarters, and paratroopers from the Rangers and the Eighty-second Airborne Division began landing at Panama City's international airport to secure that facility. Fighting raged through the night, with the PDF putting up stronger resistance than expected. Toward morning, Powell prepared to meet the press.

Shortly before 8 A.M., President Bush went on national television and explained Operation Just Cause to the American people. A few hours later, Powell met the press. By then, the worst of the fighting was over, and President Endara had been installed in the presidential palace. But Noriega was still at large, and, as Powell had predicted, the press bombarded him with questions about the dictator. Was the operation a failure because Noriega was still at large? (No. The United States had removed the dictator and restored the legitimately elected government of Panama.) Were U.S. forces in danger with Noriega running loose in the country? (No. The military was engaging in a relentless search for Noriega and would not give up until he was found.)

As it turned out, Noriega was not hiding in the jungle but had taken refuge in the Vatican embassy in Panama City, where he was seeking asylum. The papal legate, however, informed Noriega that the Pope could not grant him asylum because he was indicted on criminal charges in the United States. On January 3, 1990, Noriega realized he had no choice but to surrender to U.S. forces. He was taken immediately to Miami for trial, where he was convicted on drug charges and sentenced to life in prison.

In January, Powell visited Panama. He was grateful that only 24 U.S. soldiers had died in the fighting, four more than he had predicted. The Panama operation was a clear success, and one that followed the principles he had come to believe in during his years in the military. Unlike Vietnam, Operation Just Cause had a clear political and military objective. Also unlike Vietnam, the campaign was not micro-managed from the White House. The military professionals worked out the details and the government gave them the overwhelming force necessary to achieve the objectives. As a result, the operation was over in a couple of days, and casualties were kept low.

There were critics of Operation Just Cause. Many Americans believed it was morally wrong to intervene in the affairs of a sovereign nation. Right or wrong, the United States had a long history of intervening in the Caribbean and Central America. Powell was one of those people who believed that the national interests of the United States could not be threatened by a petty dictator who brutalized his own people and was a drug dealer to boot. The U.S. military was also criticized for the arrangements it made for the press, namely that the press was kept away from the action too long and brought in too late. Powell felt the criticism was justified and vowed to do better in the future. He would soon have the opportunity to put his promises into practice.

Chapter 9

DESERT STORM: THE WAR
TO FREE KUWAIT

On August 1, 1990, a war broke out in the Middle East. Iraq, a nation of 22 million people, invaded and occupied the neighboring country of Kuwait, on the Persian Gulf, which had a population of 1.5 million. Powell had been concerned about Iraq, which was ruled by Saddam Hussein, one of the most ruthless and cunning dictators in modern history. Between 1980 and 1988, Iraq was involved in a devastating war with the neighboring country of Iran. Since Iran was a hostile enemy of the United States, the American government supported Iraq in the conflict, selling arms to Saddam despite his record of brutality, oppression, and corruption. In retrospect, it proved to be an unwise policy.

In 1988, the Iranians agreed to end the war, which had caused millions of casualties on both sides. By the end of this bitter conflict, Iraq had an army of more than 1 million men—a dangerous force, in Powell's view, especially in the hands of the unpredictable Saddam Hussein. Between 1988 and 1990, the Iraqi government became involved in disputes with Kuwait over a variety of issues. The main one was oil, which was the principle cash-earning export of both countries. The Iraqis had a tremendous debt after the war, and they wanted to keep the price of oil high on the world market. Kuwait, according to the Iraqis, was selling oil below the price set by the Organization of Petroleum Exporting Countries (OPEC), a world oil cartel to which both countries belonged.

Another point of conflict was a large, shared oilfield that straddled the Kuwaiti-Iraqi border. The Iraqis accused Kuwait of illegally siphoning off oil to which it was not entitled. The Kuwaitis denied the charge, but Iraq kept up the drumbeat. Powell came to the conclusion that Saddam Hussein simply wanted to annex Kuwait and was creating a litany of excuses for invading its neighbor. Kuwait was much smaller than Iraq, and its population was extremely prosperous—and it had ports and shipping facilities on the Persian Gulf. That, too, made it an attractive target to the Iraqis. If Iraq could annex Kuwait and get away with it, Saddam would emerge as the most powerful and feared leader in the Middle East.

American spy satellites circling the globe had taken pictures showing that Iraqis were moving their forces to the Kuwaiti border for weeks before the invasion. By late July, some 100,000 troops were up at the Iraq-Kuwait line. But there were additional ominous signs that showed that trouble was coming. Many of the troops being moved were Saddam's elite Republican Guard units, the best of the Iraqi army. In addition, lines of communication were also being laid down, and artillery and tanks—a sure sign that an invasion was coming—were also being moved up to the border.

As soon as this intelligence became known, Powell called General H. Norman Schwarzkopf, the commander of CENTCOM (Central Command), at MacDill Air Force Base near Tampa. Since Schwarzkopf's command included the Middle East, he was responsible for coming up with military plans should the United States be forced to react. When he came to Washington in late July, Schwarzkopf predicted bluntly that the Iraqis would invade. The Bush administration, however, was not eager to get involved in conflicts between Arab states. The president hoped Arab countries would settle their own conflicts. Before the invasion, the U.S. ambassador to Iraq even urged the administration to lessen its criticism of Saddam Hussein and allow Iraq and Kuwait to work out their differences. As a result, nothing was done in late July to send a warning to Saddam Hussein that an invasion of Kuwait would be unacceptable to the United States and the world community. Some in the administration had thought of moving the aircraft carrier *Independence* into the Persian Gulf as a show of force. But before anything was done, the Iraqis made their move.

As Iraqi forces rolled into Kuwait on that August morning, Saddam Hussein proclaimed Kuwait the eighteenth province of Iraq. The emir (leader) of Kuwait fled the country. For the citizens of Kuwait, a brutal occupation was about to begin. Saddam Hussein had a justified reputation as a brutal dictator. During the war with Iran, he had used poison gas on his own people to put down an uprising of ethnic Kurds, who were agitating for independence from Iraq. He had also used chemical and biological weapons against the Iranians. Kuwait would not be treated with anything but the greatest harshness. The Iraqi soldiers engaged in wholesale looting, stealing from private homes as well as businesses, and raping Kuwaiti women. Kuwaitis were beaten in public, and some were executed. The previously neat and tidy boulevards of Kuwait City, a modern capital, were reduced to heaps of rubble and trash. Many Kuwaitis, fearing for their lives, went into hiding.

The invasion was a shock to most world leaders. Nothing this brazen had occurred in half a century, but reactions were muted in the early hours. It would take some time for the administration to decide how it wanted to respond. What was clear, however, was that the world's supply of oil—so much of it centered in the Arabian Peninsula—was now threatened. One of the world's largest suppliers, Saudi Arabia, bordered on Kuwait, and following the invasion, Iraqi troops were positioned only 40 miles from the Saudi oil fields. Forty percent of the oil used in the United States came from Saudi Arabia. If that supply were threatened, the U.S. economy would be seriously damaged.

The first meeting at the White House the day after the invasion did not produce any clear-cut decision. There was a general consensus that Saudi Arabia needed to be defended. There was great anxiety that the Iraqis would cross from Kuwait into Saudi Arabia, but no one knew for sure if this would happen. If it did, Iraq would be in a position to intimidate neighboring Arab countries like Yemen and Jordan. It would also be bad news for Israel, which had bombed an Iraqi nuclear reactor in the early 1980s to prevent Saddam Hussein from developing atomic bombs. The Iraqis had always made persistent threats to annihilate the Jewish state.

From President Bush's perspective, the most important point was that any plan to take on Iraq be done by an international coalition of nations, and that it have the United Nations' support. The president wisely understood that America could not act unilaterally in this part of the world. It was one thing for the United States to go into Panama, which was in America's backyard, but it would not be wise or possible to act alone in the Middle East, with its Islamic culture and its 40-year history of Arab-Israeli conflict. The situation was extremely delicate. The United States, with its long history of support for Israel, could not be seen as leading an anti-Arab operation.

Over the years, Powell had developed a strong personal friendship with Prince Bandar, a member of the Saudi royal family who was now the Saudi ambassador to the United States. Cheney and Powell summoned Prince Bandar to the Pentagon in order to determine the Saudi point of view about U.S. assistance against the Iraqi threat. At first, the Prince was skeptical that the United States could or would commit U.S. forces. But when Cheney and Powell said that they could guarantee at least 100,000 troops, Bandar realized the Americans were serious. But it would mean stationing American troops in Saudi Arabia in large numbers. Cheney and Schwarzkopf headed off to the Saudi capital to speak with Saudi King Fahd. On Monday, August 6, Cheney called Powell and informed him that King Fahd had agreed to the presence of American forces on Saudi soil.

In the meantime, President Bush's thinking had jelled. As he returned to the White House from the weekend at the presidential retreat at Camp David, Maryland, the president told reporters greeting his helicopter that Iraqi aggression would not stand. Powell suspected that the president was bolstered in his approach by British Prime Minister Margaret Thatcher, the "Iron Lady," who had met Bush a few days before in Aspen, Colorado. Thatcher was legendary for her uncompromising, stubborn principles and had recommended that Bush take a tough stand against the Iraqi invasion. Powell was surprised at how quickly the president had come to his decision. Now the task was to start sending U.S. forces overseas as quickly as possible. The first units to move were the Eighty-second Airborne Division in Fort Bragg, North Carolina, and the First Tactical Fighter Wing in Fort Langley, Virginia. The troops were to be moved by the Military Airlift Command (MAC), the Pentagon's airline. Orders to MAC went out on the evening of August 6, and within an hour, the first C-141 took off from Charleston Air Force Base in South Carolina headed for Saudi Arabia.

General Schwarzkopf was uneasy, however. Where was this operation going? he asked. What was the specific mission aside from providing a show of American muscle to warn Saddam and to buck up the morale of neighboring Arab states who felt threatened? Powell had to lay out the options for the president: the first troops being sent would serve as a deterrent, that is, they would be a warning to Saddam that, the Americans hoped, would make him think twice about an attack on Saudi Arabia. By December, Powell told the president, there would be more than 180,000 troops in Saudi Arabia. By this time, the mission could switch from one of deterrence to defense. That many American troops, in Powell's view, would be sufficient to defend the Saudis from an Iraqi attack.

But if the United States wanted to *remove* the Iraqis from Kuwait, Powell would need to know that by no later than October in order to keep the troops flowing into Saudi Arabia. Shortly after the Iraqi invasion in August, the United Nations had imposed a trade embargo on Iraq. These sanctions would be lifted only when Iraq withdrew its forces from Kuwait. When Powell presented his options to Bush, the president seemed doubtful that sanctions alone would ever work. This was a sign of his thinking. He wanted a complete and immediate withdrawal of Iraqi forces from

Kuwait and a restoration of the Kuwaiti government. "Complete and im-mediate," to Powell's ears, did not sound like someone who was willing to wait indefinitely for sanctions to work.

Powell asked Schwarzkopf to come up with a two-phase plan. Part one would be defensive in nature, while part two would be a plan to kick the Iraqis out of Kuwait through the use of force. After tossing about names for the plan, everyone settled on "Desert Shield" for the first phase of the plan—the buildup of forces to defend Saudi Arabia would be known as Operation Desert Shield. If an offensive against the Iraqis was approved, it would be named Operation Desert Storm. Powell's service chiefs were responsible for making sure their units were trained and ready to go over-seas. Once the units reached Saudi Arabia, they would be fully under the command of Schwarzkopf. From his office in the Saudi Ministry of De-fense, Schwarzkopf began devising a complex plan to defend Saudi Ara-bia and, if need be, attack the Iraqi army in Kuwait.

Powell, in the meantime, was consulting with the military chiefs of the countries that were part of the international coalition. Some, like Britain, France, and Arab nations on the Arabian Peninsula, were contributing military forces to the coalition. How these forces were to be used under Schwarzkopf's direction was of great concern to the military leaders of these countries as well as to their people, who were understandably anx-ious about casualties. By the fall of 1990, some 28 nations were part of the international coalition. It was a triumph for the diplomacy of President Bush and Secretary of State James Baker, who tirelessly worked the phones and, piece by piece, put together the coalition. And it was a tri-umph of Schwarzkopf's exceptional talents as a commander to blend these forces into a coherent fighting army. Schwarzkopf was able to get along exceptionally well with the Saudis. He was knowledgeable about Arab culture since he had lived in the region as a younger man. King Fahd enjoyed Schwarzkopf's company, and Prince Khalid Bin Sultan, Bandar's half-brother, was appointed commander of Arab forces in the coalition.

Powell also had to deal with the culture clash that resulted from so many American and other Western soldiers being stationed in Saudi Ara-bia, a strict Muslim country that followed Islamic law. When Powell met with his old friend Prince Bandar to go over the problems, he was flabber-gasted to learn that Bibles were prohibited in Saudi Arabia. There was no way that Americans were not going to have Bibles, so Bandar agreed to a compromise—the books would be flown into U.S. bases and not have to go through Saudi customs, where they would have been confiscated. Saudi law also prohibited Jewish religious services in the country. Powell agreed to fly Jewish military personnel to ships offshore for religious services. Alcohol was prohibited in Saudi Arabia under Islamic law, and even though its absence led to bitter complaints on the part of the Westerners, it probably led to fewer discipline problems since no one had the opportunity to get drunk.

Then there was the issue of Western women in Saudi Arabia. American women were an integral part of the U.S. military. They drove vehicles and wore clothing that exposed their arms and heads. Under Islamic law, Saudi women were required to wear the head scarf and to cover their arms. And they were not allowed to drive. As soon as some Saudi women saw the American women behind the wheels of vehicles, they demanded the right to drive for themselves. It was a source of tension, a symbol of a cultural clash that would haunt America's relations with Arab Middle Eastern countries then and into the future. (One disaffected and wealthy Saudi became so incensed by the presence of American soldiers on the holy Islamic soil of Saudi Arabia that he devoted the rest of his life to ridding his country of the infidel. The man, Osama bin Laden, began a career of terrorism against the United States that was to include attacks on American interests abroad and in the United States itself on September 11, 2001. [See chapter 12.])

Air power was a key element in any war against Iraq. To come up with an air campaign, Schwarzkopf selected a brilliant young colonel named John Warden. A fighter pilot by training, Warden was an ardent believer in air power. He recommended relentless bombing of Iraqi communications and defense systems (especially radar), command and control facilities that directed the Iraqi army in the field, and transportation, storage, and production facilities—all within Iraq.

For a potential ground campaign, Schwarzkopf assembled a group of young lieutenant colonels that came to be known as the "Jedi Knights." The Jedi Knights created the plan for a ground campaign that would expel the Iraqi military from Kuwait. The ground plan, however, took some time to come together. The major reason was that no one knew for sure how many troops President Bush would eventually commit to the campaign. The 180,000 or so in Saudi Arabia were not enough for an offensive into Iraq. This uncertainty was extremely frustrating to Schwarzkopf, who insisted he would need at least several divisions to conduct a successful mission. Powell kept assuring him that he would eventually get what he needed, and that the president would not make him fight a war without every possible resource he needed to win.

Privately, Powell was concerned that the president was coming to believe that an air campaign alone could do the job. Powell—and Cheney—

did not believe this for a minute. They understood that a large commitment of ground troops and tanks from America and other nations was needed to expel the Iraqi army from Kuwait. Several versions of a ground campaign were discussed, and each time Powell told the men to go back to the drawing boards and come up with something better. The number of troops available was surely an issue. But what was the overall strategy? How were the troops to be used in battle?

Decision day was October 30, 1990. The president and his advisers met in the Situation Room of the White House to discuss the war plan. Powell presented the plan to the gathered officials. It would begin with an extended air campaign designed to destroy Iraqi command and communications centers. After several weeks of pounding, the ground war would begin. Powell and Schwarzkopf believed it was important to take advantage of the static position of the Iraqi forces in Kuwait. They were dug in facing the Saudi border and as a result were not terribly mobile. The U.S. strategy would include a frontal assault on these lines, preceded by a feint campaign to trick the Iraqis into thinking that the U.S. was invading Kuwait from the Persian Gulf. While the Iraqis were focused on the attack on their front lines, U.S. forces would sweep into Iraq from the west in a wide arc, trapping the Iraqi army in Kuwait from the rear.

It was a brilliant tactical plan. How many troops would it take? Before Powell answered, the president leaned forward expectantly. The answer was startling: as many as 500,000, more than double the amount expected in Saudi Arabia by December of 1990. It would mean moving units from Germany and the addition of another Marine division. Six aircraft carriers were to be positioned in the Persian Gulf, their planes at the ready to attack wherever they were sent.

The coalition assembled by President Bush was in a solid position to contribute to the effort. An additional 200,000 troops, many from Great Britain, would supplement the 500,000 Americans. Arab troops from other nations in the Persian Gulf region would form the advance units entering Kuwait from Saudi Arabia. And Egypt and Saudi Arabia together would be contributing some 50,000 troops. On the diplomatic front, it was essential that Israel, America's strongest ally in the region, not get involved in the conflict. It was inconceivable for Arab countries to fight against another Arab country with Israel on their side. Even if they were attacked, the Israelis could not become combatants of any kind. This would be an incredibly difficult goal to achieve, since the Israelis, throughout their brief history as a nation, had never allowed any kind of attack on their country to go unanswered without some form of retaliation.

Further diplomatic backing for the war against Iraq came in November, when the United Nations passed Resolution 678 calling for the use of "all means necessary" to free Kuwait from occupation. The Soviets voted for the resolution. It was a historic moment—the United States and the Soviet Union were on the same side in a major international dispute for the first time since World War II.

The mission was to expel the Iraqi army from Kuwait and liberate that country. It was not to overthrow Saddam Hussein, however despicable he was as a dictator. Despite the limited nature of the offensive, members of Congress were nervous, and some opposed going to war before giving sanctions a chance to work. Powell appeared before the Senate Armed Services Committee, headed by the influential Democrat from Georgia, Senator Sam Nunn. Nunn, an expert in national defense and military matters, did not want to go to war. He and other opponents pointed out that there were 450,000 Iraqi troops in Kuwait, as well as 3,800 tanks, and 2,500 artillery pieces. The Iraqis also had short-range missiles—SCUDS—that they threatened to fire into Israeli cities. Powell was honest with the senators—it was not going to be an easy job, but it had to be done.

The most fearful weapons in the Iraqi military, however, were their chemical and biological weapons. What was to prevent them from using these dreadful weapons on Americans? As far as anyone knew, the answer was nothing. American troops were fitted with protective gear to shield them from most chemical weapons. In addition, they would be moving in protected vehicles such as tanks and armored personnel carriers. Biological agents, however, were a big unknown. The bombing plan called for the destruction of known chemical and biological facilities. Would clouds of germs be sent floating over the coalition forces as a result of this bombing? And what if Saddam intentionally used these agents? Powell made sure that the Iraqis were informed, in no uncertain terms, that the United States planned to wage a conventional war. If terrible chemical and germ weapons were used, however, the United States would exact a terrible retribution. Although probably a bluff, Powell let it be known then that dams on the Tigris and Euphrates rivers would be bombed, unleashing devastating floods on the Iraqi capital of Baghdad. But the trump card—which was never stated but was implied, both by Powell and Secretary of State Baker—was that the Iraqis faced a nuclear attack if they dared to use chemical or biological weapons.

Throughout November and December, the buildup continued. Desert Shield was a monumental logistical challenge. The shipment of hundreds of thousands of troops, artillery, tanks, support materials, food, and countless other items were in the able hands of Lieutenant General Gus

Pagonas. The logistics people rarely appeared in the headlines, but without them, the offensive could not occur. The sheer size of the effort was illustrated by one simple example: by Christmas of 1990, three C-5 Galaxies a day—the largest transports in the fleet—were flying to Saudi Arabia filled only with mail or Christmas presents for the troops from their families.

By early January 1991, the final countdown to war had begun. Before the guns started firing, Secretary of State Baker flew to Geneva, Switzerland, to meet with Iraqi foreign minister Tariq Aziz. The Iraqis seemed totally unwilling to budge, even as the UN-imposed deadline for withdrawal from Kuwait (January 15) approached. It seemed astonishing to Powell that the Iraqis would willingly go to war, when it was so clear they were facing the might of one of the greatest coalitions in the world. It dawned on Powell that a regime that used poison gas on its own people was not terribly concerned about the reality that tens of thousands of its own soldiers would most certainly die.

Powell also noticed that Bush seemed eager to get on with it. The tension in Washington was rising, both in and out of the administration. Some members of the House of Representatives filed a federal lawsuit trying to prevent President Bush from waging war without a congressional declaration. And both houses of Congress were preparing to vote on a resolution authorizing the president to wage war on Iraq. Some in the White House were afraid that the resolution would be defeated, which would then have placed the president in an impossibly embarrassing position. Powell felt going after a resolution of support was a good idea, even at the risk of failure. From his perspective, it was important that the Congress of the United States—the people's legislature—be publicly behind America's men and women as they went into battle. A few days before the expiration of the UN deadline, the Congress passed a resolution requiring the president to report that all efforts to get Iraq to comply with the UN resolutions had failed before hostilities began. This was, in effect, the support Bush had hoped for, a recognition on the part of Congress that the United States would be going to war shortly.

Powell observed how each leader handled the growing pressure differently. Schwarzkopf, the man responsible for managing the war on the front lines, had a volatile, excitable personality. When he was not happy with something, Powell was the first one to get the phone call. Cheney, in contrast, always seemed cool and collected, a man who listened, questioned, and then made up his mind in an atmosphere of calm. President Bush had the capacity to make people feel at ease. As the hour of war approached, the president was somber and clearly deeply aware of the fact that the order to begin hostilities—his order—would lead to American casualties.

Everyone was concerned about casualties and assumed the worst. Newspapers were carrying stories of 15,000 body bags being shipped to the Middle East in anticipation of staggering battlefield deaths. Privately, Powell expected about 5,000 casualties, and although he did not say so publicly, he did not believe the high estimates but remained hopeful that the number of deaths and injuries would be on the low side. He had faith in American technology and preparedness, but most important, in the young American men and women who would be waging the battle for Kuwait's liberation.

On January 15, 1991, the UN deadline came and went, and Saddam Hussein still refused to pull his forces out of Iraq. The administration had decided a few days before that the bombing would begin in the pre-dawn hours of January 17, Iraq time, which would be the evening of January 16 in Washington. At that time, Powell was sitting in his office watching CNN, whose correspondents in Baghdad were reporting that the Iraqis were firing into the dark sky over the city. Powell knew what was happening. Cruise missiles fired from American ships in the Persian Gulf and from B-52s over Iraq were smashing into Iraqi installations all over the country. B-117A Stealth fighters from Saudi Arabia and Navy A-6s launched from aircraft carriers attacked government and military sites. Closer to Kuwait, Apache helicopters flew into Iraqi airspace and obliterated early warning radar facilities. In addition, hundreds of aircraft from coalition countries attacked pre-selected targets all over Iraq. A massive, coordinated air assault was under way that would blast Iraq for weeks before any ground war began.

At the end of the first day of the air campaign, Schwarzkopf called Powell to report. The results were wildly successful beyond all expectations. The Iraqi air defenses had melted almost without opposition in the face of the tremendous attack. Command and communications installations had taken a tremendous hit. TV viewers saw the night skies over Baghdad aglow with tracers as hundreds of antiaircraft rounds were fired. But it was in vain. They were firing blindly into the sky and were hitting nothing. It was a fireworks display that amounted to a total waste of ammunition. Powell was concerned that the media were feeding into a premature sense of victory. A war was not won on the basis of one day of bombing. And the Iraqis still had a powerful army on the ground and stockpiles of chemical and biological weapons.

Powell felt it was necessary for the administration to provide its own position on the war and not to let the media be the sole interpreter of what was happening. With Cheney's approval, Schwarzkopf and Powell decided to hold a joint news conference on January 23, 1991. Powell would present the view from Washington. In Saudi Arabia, Schwarzkopf would be the principal briefer. Schwarzkopf was especially good on TV. An essentially hot medium, television tends to exaggerate physical characteristics. As a result, "Stormin' Norman," a colorful individual in the flesh, was even more so on TV. The public loved him, with his charts, pointer, and pithy comments. Powell, in contrast, was cool, confident, and cerebral. The almost-daily news conferences Powell had during the Persian Gulf War was the first time Americans saw him up close during a time of crisis. And they liked what they saw. Powell became a truly international figure in 1991. At this first news conference in January 1991, Powell uttered a phrase that made an enormous impact. When characterizing U.S. strategy regarding the Iraqi army, Powell said: "First, we are going to cut it off, then we are going to kill it."[1] The phrase was widely quoted that evening on TV news shows and the next day in the newspapers. Although some in the government were nervous about the use of the word "kill," Powell felt it was a clear and unambiguous statement about the military objectives of the United States.

Technology allowed Americans to see unique images of war. Cameras built into cruise missiles showed the journey to the target right up to the moment of impact. State-of-the-art cameras in fighter aircraft showed Iraqi installations at the moment the missiles struck them. One famous shot showed a car as it raced across a bridge over the Tigris River, escaping just moments before a missile demolished the span. Another tape, narrated colorfully by Schwarzkopf in Saudi Arabia, showed a missile as it dropped directly on the headquarters of the Iraqi air force in Baghdad.

But not all the images caused Americans to cheer. On February 13, two aircraft scored a hit on a bunker in Baghdad that the U.S. military believed was a command center. It may have been, but the Iraqis were also using it as a civilian shelter. Images of dozens of dead women and children being pulled from the demolished bunker flashed all over the world. These kinds of pictures were damaging to the coalition cause and created sympathy for the Iraqi people, who Saddam portrayed as victims of cruel and indiscriminate bombing.

Another strain on the coalition was the desire of Israel to strike at Iraq. Shortly after the air campaign began, the Iraqis fired SCUD missiles on the Israeli cities of Tel Aviv and Haifa. SCUDs were military hardware that had been acquired from the Soviet Union years before. They were notoriously inaccurate and clumsy, and they had a very short range. But from the point of view of the Iraqis, it didn't matter. They just pointed them at Israeli cities, and any place they fell was good enough. By attacking Israel, Iraq hoped to provoke the Israelis into attacking them, thus disrupting the coalition.

Powell, Bush, and Baker worked hard to restrain the understandable desire on the part of the Israelis to attack SCUD sites in Iraq. Reluctantly, the Israelis agreed in return for U.S. Patriot missiles, which were used to intercept the SCUDs before they struck the ground. Although far from perfect in their performance, the Patriots made the Israelis feel more secure and kept the Israelis out of the war.

The stresses being placed on the coalition by the air phase of the war made President Bush impatient to get on with the ground offensive. The original date for the land attack was February 21. But Schwarzkopf, on the recommendation of his marine general in charge of the divisions that would be charging the Iraqi fortifications, urged a delay of a few days. Bush reluctantly agreed to a postponement to February 24. When Schwarkopf asked for another delay, Powell refused, and the two got into a yelling match over the telephone. In the end, Schwarzkopf agreed to abide by the February 24 date.

The plan that had been originally agreed to was activated. The marines as well as Egyptian, Syrian, Saudi and other Arab units went directly against the Iraqi forces that were entrenched on the Kuwait border. Their mission was not necessarily to crack these lines, but to distract the Iraqis and hold them down while U.S. and coalition forces attacked Iraq's exposed western flank, driving into the desert and trapping the Iraqi army in Kuwait—and killing them. The major part of the flanking maneuver was to be done by a combined force known as the VII Corps under Lieutenant General Fred Franks. Many other units, including parts of the Eighty-second Airborne Division, attacked Iraq directly, driving north toward the Euphrates River.

Powell stayed in his office all night watching CNN and receiving reports from the front. The Iraqi fortifications on the Kuwait-Saudi line seemed insurmountable. In addition to anti-tank trenches, the Iraqi army had erected booby-trapped barbed wire, placed thousands of mines, and dug ditches that would be filled with flaming oil. But, as Powell watched from Washington, the marines and the coalition forces did more than just pin the Iraqis down. They penetrated the fortifications almost immediately and were halfway to Kuwait City in the first day of fighting. To the west, advanced units moved 60 miles into Iraq. By the second day, the marines were fighting at Kuwait City International Airport and had captured more than 10,000 Iraqi soldiers. By nightfall, Kuwait City was encircled.

On the third day, Kuwait City was liberated. Powell and Schwarzkopf, while ecstatic over the progress of the ground campaign, were concerned, however, that General Franks was not moving his VII Corps fast enough to engage Iraqi Republican Guards that were fleeing northward. Schwarzkopf kept pressuring, and on that day the VII Corps made contact with and destroyed a Republican Guards division in a massive tank battle. The Iraqi prisoners in coalition custody grew in leaps and bounds. After three days, more than 70,000 were in custody. U.S. intelligence believed that 27 of the 42 Iraqi divisions in the combat zone had been destroyed or severely damaged. U.S. casualties were light—only eight in combat after the first day—although a SCUD missile hit a barracks in Saudi Arabia killing 28 U.S. soldiers. Friendly fire—U.S. artillery and aircraft fire that accidentally hit American soldiers—also accounted for several dozen deaths.

But once again, dreadful images on TV influenced events. Iraqi vehicles fleeing Kuwait toward the city of Basrah jammed the one four-lane highway north out of the country. U.S. air power attacked the convoy, which consisted of tanks as well as military and civilian vehicles. The casualties were staggering. American TV viewers—including Bush and Powell—saw pictures of hundreds of destroyed vehicles and charred corpses on the road, which the media named the "highway of death." The Iraqis, by and large, had been removed from Kuwait. Would the world now think that the coalition was engaging in killing Iraqis just for the sake of killing?

Even before these stark images appeared on TV, Powell had been thinking about how to end the war. Generals, he was acutely aware, spend most of their time thinking of how to start wars, not how to end them. On the afternoon of February 27, President Bush and his advisers met in the Oval Office. Powell had spoken earlier in the day to Schwarzkopf, who said that he would need one more day to finish the job. Bush and a number of other advisers, including Secretary of State Baker, were concerned that the United States not be seen as vengeful killers. The carnage on the highway to Basrah might hurt the image of the United States and the coalition. Bush asked if the war could be stopped now, instead of the following day. Powell called Schwarzkopf, who didn't have a problem with a cessation of hostilities sooner rather than later in the following day. After additional meetings, it was agreed that the president would address the nation at 9 P.M. that evening and announce the end of hostilities for 8 A.M. the following morning, Kuwait time. In his address to the country, the president stressed that the coalition had met its objective—the liberation of Kuwait and the restoration of its legitimate government.

For Powell, there was never any question that the United States would exceed its mandate and go all the way to Baghdad to overthrow Saddam Hussein. He would never have advised such an action, and he strongly defended the ending of the war after three days. In the months and years to follow, the continued presence of Saddam on the world scene would be debated, long after Bush and his successor had left the presidency and into the presidency of his son, George W. Bush. But on the night of February 27, 1991, there were no doubts. Right after the president's address, Powell and a small group of advisers were invited to join the president and Mrs. Bush in the residence at the White House for drinks. Powell remembered that everyone felt relieved more than happy at the victory. The president and Powell believed they had done the right thing. The "100-Hour War" had propelled George Bush to new heights of popularity. But it had also made Colin Powell a household name, a popular international figure whose calm and integrity were widely admired.

NOTE

1. Powell, *My American Journey*, p. 495.

Chapter 10

AFTER THE STORM: FINAL YEARS IN THE MILITARY

No sooner was the Persian Gulf War over than commentators and politicians began critiquing the conflict. The debates that arose were driven in part by the disappointing reality that Saddam Hussein, despite the heavy losses sustained by his army and the terrible suffering of his people, remained in power. The decision not to overthrow his government was a political one, made in the end by President George Bush. But Powell had supported Bush totally—and in fact had recommended the ending of hostilities after three days. In the years after the war, the subject never seemed to go away. One prominent journalist referred to Powell as the reluctant warrior, reporting incorrectly that Powell had counseled the president not to go to war. Powell resented this portrayal of himself and always strongly defended the policies of the administration. American casualties in the war had not been in the thousands, as was feared—in no small case because the United States and its allies knew when to end the conflict. In the end, 147 Americans died in combat and another 236 died from accidents and other causes. Powell was truly grateful for this low number and was proud of the American military—for its preparedness, its excellent equipment, and its outstanding young men and women.

With the Gulf War over, Powell was confident that the defeat of Iraqi aggression would have a beneficial effect on the peace process between Israel and its Arab neighbors. He hoped that the defeat of Saddam Hussein would make moderate Arabs more amenable to peace with the Israelis. This, however, did not happen, and a decade later, when Powell was back in government as Secretary of State, he would be dealing with the ever-present torment of Israeli-Arab conflict, as had all of his predecessors for the preceding 50 years.

But in the early weeks of 1991, it was a time of celebration—of parades, of honors, of praise, and of the announcement of Powell's early reappointment to another two-year term as chairman. The country wanted to savor the victory, especially since the tortured years of Vietnam. Powell and Schwarzkopf were treated to a ticker-tape parade through the streets of lower Manhattan in New York City.

A month before Powell began his second term; one of the most momentous events in twentieth-century history began to unfold. In August 1991, a group of hard-line old Communists in the Soviet Union attempted to overthrow Mikhail Gorbachev. For three days, Gorbachev and his family were held under house arrest at his summer residence on the Black Sea. But the Russian people inspired by the president of the Russian Republic, Boris Yeltsin, refused to accept a military coup. After 72 hours, during which ordinary people faced down tanks in the street, the rebellion collapsed and Gorbachev returned to Moscow.

Powell had long believed that Gorbachev, the reformer, would ratchet down the arms race and that the new, lean (and poor) Soviet Union would be a lion without its teeth. What he did not predict, however, was the total collapse of the Soviet Union and the fracturing of the former country into numerous independent states. The coup spelled the doom of the Communist Party in the USSR, but it was also the end for Gorbachev and the rise of Yeltsin. In December 1991, the Soviet Union disbanded itself, and Gorbachev was out a job. The largest republic to emerge from the former USSR was Russia, with Yeltsin as its president.

As the Soviet Union was disintegrating, President Bush asked his advisers for a new initiative on nuclear arms. Powell had long urged the elimination of small, artillery-based nuclear weapons—a proposal the army bitterly resisted. But now, in the wake of the Gulf War and the death throes of the Soviet Union, Powell and Bush's national security team offered far more radical, unilateral cuts in the U.S. nuclear arsenal. The proposal called for the elimination of short-range nuclear weapons; the grounding of bombers that carried nuclear weapons that had been on round-the-clock alert for more than 30 years; and the elimination of certain kinds of intercontinental ballistic missiles. The program, when taken together with the START treaties negotiated with the USSR in the 1980s, would mean a 65 percent reduction in the total number of nuclear weapons in the U.S. arsenal. Powell was rightly proud of this astonishing achievement, which helped make the world safe from nuclear annihilation.

Cutting nuclear weapons proved easy, however, when compared with trying to reduce the size of the military and close unneeded bases. Powell was aware that in the past, cuts in the military had often been made without a coherent plan. This time, however, Bush, Cheney, and Powell had thought long and hard about where the reductions could be made. Powell had always been aware that he was a trustee of the taxpayers' money. He believed it was his responsibility to spend that money wisely and not to waste billions of dollars on unnecessary armaments, personnel, or military installations.

The military, however, is one of the largest employers in the country, not only of people in uniform but of the countless numbers who work in the civilian economy that supports defense industries. As a result, any cut in military spending would mean a loss of jobs—military and civilian. And unemployment always spells bad news for politicians. Many members of Congress would be more than willing to criticize military spending—except when it came to cutting defense spending in their home districts.

As much as Powell disliked this aspect of the process, he knew very well that he would have to dance very carefully around the issue of cuts in the military if anything were to get through Congress. The administration started with the easy cuts—in Europe. With the end of the Cold War, the United States no longer needed to keep hundreds of thousands of troops in Germany. Powell had a nostalgic feeling when he approved the closing of the army base at Gelnhausen, his first overseas posting in the 1950s. Members of Congress had no problems with the cuts in Europe—Germans didn't vote in American elections.

But the reductions in the United States were more difficult. The National Guard and the reserves, for example, had grown from 250,000 to more than 1 million under Reagan. The guard and the reserves that were called up to duty during the Persian Gulf War had performed heroically. But, as Powell understood, there was simply no longer the need for that many of them.

Another contentious issue was military bases in the United States. A prime example was Loring Air Force Base in northern Maine. It had been created during the era when long-range bombers needed a base to refuel on their way to Europe and the Soviet Union to fight a mythical World War III. By the 1990s, Loring was a total anachronism. But its location—in extreme northern Maine—was in a poor part of the state, on the border with Canada. The region was heavily wooded and had almost no other source of income. Close Loring, and you put the surrounding population on the list of the permanently unemployed. (Loring was ultimately shut down; its facilities were turned over to the state of Maine, and some of them were converted into a magnet school for gifted high school students.)

In order to placate Congress, a commission was created to review suggested Pentagon closings every two years. It had been established when Frank Carlucci was Secretary of Defense, and even though Powell found the entire process distasteful, he realized he had to go along with it. This was the reality of life in a democracy. During his tenure as chairman, Powell and his team put forward a plan to reduce military spending and to modernize the force to make it lean and efficient and prepared to fight the wars of the twenty-first century. Some parts were accepted, others were rejected.

By the spring of 1992, Powell became aware that President Bush's reelection prospects were in trouble. The high popularity ratings Bush had enjoyed in 1991 at the end of the Gulf War had slipped away as the economy went into a recession. Bush also seemed at times aloof and reluctant to campaign for the job. In May 1992, race riots broke out in Los Angeles after a jury acquitted white policemen who had beaten an African American motorist, Rodney King—a beating captured on tape. Powell was distressed, first at Bush's slow response, then at a draft of a speech in which the president condemned the rioting but made no mention of the social ills underlying the riots or the injustice that blacks felt toward the acquittals. Although the final speech was modified on Powell's suggestion, he remained concerned about the advice the president was getting.

At the Republican National Convention in August 1992, Bush was renominated, but his sinking standings in the polls led to rumors that he would dump his vice president, Dan Quayle, and replace him with a more popular figure. Powell's name was mentioned, which was deeply embarrassing to him. He craved no political position, and he did not want Bush or Quayle to think he was behind these rumors. Powell knew that Bush was extremely loyal to his subordinates and that he had no intention of replacing Quayle. In the end, Quayle was also renominated, but the convention as a whole—with incendiary speeches by right-wing Republicans—damaged Bush even more.

Republicans had not been the only ones interested in a possible Powell candidacy. Some Democrats, as well, thought he would make an excellent Democratic vice presidential candidate. Powell had to point out to them that he was not interested in elective politics, and even if he were, he would never stand against a president who had advanced his career and befriended him. Besides, Powell had helped create the national security policies over the last 10 years. Was he now supposed to take off his uniform and run against his own record? The idea was preposterous.

On November 3, 1992, Bush was soundly defeated by Governor Bill Clinton of Arkansas. The weekend after the election, Bush invited Colin and Alma to Camp David for the weekend. Powell was surprised by the invitation, assuming that the president would have preferred to be alone with his family in the wake of his loss. But, as Barbara Bush explained, they wanted to be with real friends at this time. Powell was deeply touched. Here was a man who had suffered a crushing defeat, yet he was still able to reach out and, in a way, comfort his friends. Powell realized and appreciated the strength of his friendship with the Bush family.

The final months of the Bush administration offered no let-up in foreign policy problems. In Haiti, a coup had overthrown the elected government, and refugees were pouring into the United States on makeshift boats. To stem the tide, the government sent the refugees to the U.S. Naval base at Guantánamo Bay, Cuba, where they were interviewed and the genuine political refugees then sent on to the United States. In Bosnia, in the former Yugoslavia, Muslims by the thousands were being murdered by Serbs, and the pressure on Bush was strong to use American force to end the conflict. Powell was opposed to any mission that was not clearly defined and that lacked an entrance and exit strategy. Bosnia was a civil war and therefore a quagmire. He urged the president not to intervene and took some criticism in the press for not being willing to use American power to help stop genocide. The third problem area that emerged in these final months of 1992 was in Somalia, in East Africa. There, starvation resulting from a deadly civil conflict was decimating the population. President Bush wanted to send in American troops for humanitarian reasons and then make sure they were out before Clinton took office on January 20, 1993. Powell and Cheney both told the president frankly that it would not be possible to be in and out in a month. Ultimately, 24,500 Americans went to Somalia in what started out as a humanitarian mission but then ended in nation building during the Clinton administration—and in American casualties.

Shortly after the election, President-elect Clinton asked to meet Powell. They met in a hotel in Washington, and Powell was struck by Clinton's extraordinary intelligence and ability to absorb the details of complex issues. The two could not have had a more different experience with regard to military service. Clinton, a child of the 1960s, had not served in the military. In fact, during the election his opponents had accused him of being a draft dodger during the Vietnam War, and the evidence suggested that Clinton had taken actions to avoid the draft without making it appear that he had done so.

Two things made Powell uneasy about the meeting. One was Clinton's suggestion that he wanted to remove the ban on gay people from serving in the military. The ban had been imposed during the administration of Ronald Reagan to appease the right wing of the Republican Party. Powell urged the president to go slow on this issue, knowing that there would be enormous opposition to the change in the military itself and in Congress. He suggested that the president appoint a commission to study the subject and that Clinton not start his administration by pushing a controversial social issue. Clinton did not say what he would do. Powell also felt uncomfortable when Clinton asked for his assessment of three candidates Clinton was considering for Secretary of Defense. Powell didn't feel like giving opinions on someone who might soon be his boss. From the way Clinton spoke, Powell believed that he had already decided on Representative Les Aspin. A Ph.D. from MIT, Aspin was a brilliant man who had an enormous knowledge of defense issues but with whom Powell had clashed on a number of occasions when testifying before Congress.

Bill Clinton was about to be the new commander in chief and Powell assured him of his loyalty. Powell realized that he would be a major holdover from the previous administration, and that Clinton might want to have his own man as chairman as soon as possible. Powell told Clinton that he would be willing to leave before the expiration of his term in September 1993, but Clinton said no, he wanted Powell to stay on.

Shortly after the inauguration, Powell and his service chiefs were summoned to the White House for a meeting. At the table were the president, Vice President Al Gore, and numerous aides. After a review of the status and needs of each of the services, the president brought up the subject of gays in the military. He felt he had made a campaign promise to remove this ban. The service chiefs explained that there was almost universal opposition to it among the people in the military. Powell expressed his reservation, saying that the issue came down to one of privacy, that the difficulties that would arise on issues of fraternization, accommodations, and morale in general could be disruptive. He again urged the president not to make it an immediate issue in the early days of his administration. Clinton agreed with the latter advice and decided to hold off on an announcement.

The next day, several newspapers and magazines carried articles that Powell had vehemently opposed the lifting of the ban on gays and had almost been insubordinate to the president. Powell was stunned and hurt by the articles. He had given the president his best advice, but he had not been insubordinate. Whatever the president decided, he would support and carry out as any loyal soldier would. But for years afterward, Powell took heavy criticism for his stand on this issue. Critics pointed out that many of the same arguments used to keep gays out of the military had been used 40 years earlier to justify segregation in the military. At that time, President Harry Truman issued an executive order abolishing segregation in all the armed forces. Powell disagreed with the analogy. Skin color was not a matter of choice in life—you cannot hide your race. Being gay, however, was a behavioral issue (in Powell's view) and as such was much more complex and difficult to deal with.

Powell told Clinton that he was well aware that gay people were already in the military and were serving honorably. But because of the official ban, gay people were hidden. This reality became the basis of the policy eventually adopted by the Clinton administration. Powell suggested to the president that the question "Are you a homosexual?" simply not be asked when a person enlisted. That change was put into effect immediately. The policy change that was finally approved was dubbed "Don't ask, don't tell." Gay people could serve in the military as long as they did not reveal they were gay. Men or women would no longer be asked about their sexual orientation on enlistment. But if they announced openly that they were gay once they were in uniform, they would be dismissed from active duty.

The changes did not satisfy gay activists, who did not want gays to have to hide their sexuality, and they angered conservatives, who wanted to leave the ban in place. Powell was shaken by the public beating he took on the issue. The gay controversy was only one of the events that made Powell's final year in office difficult. Another was the shift from Cheney to Aspin and his dealings with the White House staff.

The change from Cheney to Aspin was a major shift in styles of leadership. Cheney was organized, structured, and predictable. Aspin, in contrast, was disorganized and prone to go off on tangents. Aspin looked like an absentminded professor. His meetings at the Pentagon were more like college bull sessions, with everyone expressing an opinion and talking at once, and with all subsequent meetings running behind schedule. Meetings at the White House were not that much different. Powell was stunned to hear second- or third-level staffers, who traditionally sat silently along the wall taking notes, interrupt cabinet-level speakers to express their opinions. For a military man, the breakdown of order and hierarchy—and with its underlying impudence—was hard to take. But more important, in Powell's view, good decisions rarely came out of a chaotic environment. Powell recognized that Clinton, like Aspin, came from an academic background, and as a former law school professor, he was used to meetings where ideas were tossed about in freewheeling gabfests. Through it all, he could see—and respect—Clinton's great intelligence, political skills, and commitment to doing a good job for the country.

At times, Powell felt he had to defend the president. When Clinton was scheduled to speak on Memorial Day 1993 at the Vietnam Memorial in Washington, many veterans groups protested. They did not feel that it was appropriate for a draft dodger to appear at a memorial honoring the nation's dead. Powell was upset by that point of view. Clinton may have avoided the draft, but so had many thousands of young men of that era. It was no big deal anymore, especially since the American people had rejected it as an issue in the 1992 campaign. More important to Powell was the fact that Bill Clinton was the nation's commander in chief and was due the respect inherent in that office. When he introduced Clinton to the crowd, he specifically used those words. The applause exceeded a smattering of boos. Clinton later thanked him for the introduction, realizing that Powell had used his prestige as a kind of shield to protect the president from angry protestors.

In those final months as chairman, Powell could see that a number of policies were veering in dangerous directions. The Somalia mission, which had begun in George Bush's final days in office, was, under UN prodding, becoming one that involved U.S. troops in the country's political tribal wars. Nation building—in Powell's view an impossible task and a totally inappropriate use of U.S. forces—was exactly what Vietnam was supposed to have been, with horrific consequences. But slowly, more and more troops were sent to Somalia, drawing the United States into the civil war that had decimated that poverty-stricken land. Powell had been opposed to U.S. involvement, but when a commander on the ground in Somalia asked for tanks to defend his troops, Powell said yes. But this time, Aspin, who was also opposed to increasing U.S. involvement, said no. A few weeks later, 18 Americans were killed in a mission that later became the subject of the movie *Black Hawk Down*. Aspin was severely criticized for refusing the request for tanks, and within a few months, Clinton asked him to resign. Powell had been opposed to the mission, but he also believed once the troops were in place, they needed all the support the country could give them.

In the Balkans, many people in the administration were pushing for U.S. involvement to end the mass murder taking place in Bosnia. UN ambassador Madeleine Albright pushed for U.S. troops in the former Yugoslavia. She wanted to know why we had this superb military if we were not willing to use it? The question greatly angered Powell, who explained to her that the U.S. military was not a toy that could be used thought-lessly. The argument was a classic confrontation between a cautious military commander and a diplomat who was genuinely concerned about the atrocities taking place in the former Yugoslavia. (After Powell left office, the United States and its NATO allies waged a ferocious air campaign against Serbia because of its ethnic cleansing of Albanians in the province of Kosovo.)

September 30, 1993 was Colin Powell's last day in the military. The Defense Department planned an elaborate farewell ceremony on the parade grounds of Fort Myer, Virginia. On the morning of the thirtieth, Powell was summoned to the White House by the president. Clinton just wanted to thank Powell personally for his service. The two sat on the Truman balcony overlooking the Washington Monument as Clinton inquired if Powell would be interested in any special assignments. Powell said he wanted some time off but would consider anything the president requested. Later that afternoon, the President and Mrs. Clinton, along with former President Bush, members of the administration, the top brass at the Pentagon, and many members of the extended Powell family gathered at Fort Myer. The president presented Powell with the Presidential Medal of Freedom with Distinction (an upgrade of the Presidential Medal of Freedom, which Powell had received a year earlier). Powell was content during the ceremony to know that his successor was a man of distinction and ability: John M. Shalikashvili, who was born and raised in Warsaw, Poland, and who came to the United States in his teens and still spoke with a slight accent. His story, like Powell's, was a shining example of how the U.S. military offered untold opportunities to young men and women not born into privilege—or even in the country.

With the ceremony over, Powell and Alma returned home. For the last time, he took off his uniform. His career of 35 years in the military was now history. On that day, however, he could not have imagined what fate still had in store for him.

Chapter 11

CITIZEN POWELL: POLITICS AND THE PRIVATE WORLD

Colin Powell had mixed feelings about leaving the military. He probably could have had another two-year term as chairman of the Joint Chiefs of Staff, but he decided not to ask for it. Although he believed he had a good relationship with the president, he knew there were plenty of people in the Clinton administration who were glad to see him go. And he understood why. As a confidant of President Bush, he always felt somewhat like an outsider among Clinton's advisers. Besides, he now felt it was time to earn some money for his family. Powell prepared to write an autobiography and to give speeches around the country—a great way to make money quickly.

But the transition was not easy, and often amusing things happened to underline that he was now Mr. Powell, not General Powell. When the kitchen sink in his new house near Washington developed a leak, Powell's first thought was to call the base maintenance people—until he realized there no were base plumbers available for him. When driving one of his favorite old Volvos that he had faithfully restored (restoring old cars was one of Powell's great passions), he was embarrassed to run out of gas on the highway. The motorcycle cop who came to his rescue didn't recognize Powell, whose face was partially hidden by a baseball cap, and gave him a good-natured lecture on the importance of checking your tank before you leave home. But daily life was also peaceful and easygoing and was an enjoyable contrast after years at the center of power. There were evenings of quiet reading, movies, or just watching TV. The children were all grown and on their own, so visits to them had a special enjoyment.

In December of 1993 Powell received a very special honor, one that he wished his parents had lived to see. That month, he was knighted by

Queen Elizabeth II of Great Britain. Powell and Alma appeared before the Queen in Buckingham Palace as he was made a Knight Commander of the Order of Bath. "Sir Colin" may have seemed an amusing honorary title for an American from the Bronx, but Powell couldn't help thinking of his mother and father, who had come to the United States bearing the British passports carried by Jamaicans at that time. They had always been so proud of the British part of their Jamaican heritage and would have been thrilled to see their son honored by the Queen of England.

As a distinguished former general, Powell was sometimes asked to undertake specific assignments for the president. In 1994, he joined a delegation of Americans to attend the inauguration of Nelson Mandela as president of South Africa. Mandela had spent nearly 30 years in prison because of his opposition to South Africa's policy of strict racial segregation known as apartheid. But by the early 1990s, the white South African government realized it had to get rid of apartheid if it was to be free of UN-mandated sanctions and if it wanted to join the world community as a respected nation. Mandela was freed from prison, and just a few short years later, he was elected president of a South Africa in which blacks voted for the first time and took up the same liberties and privileges as whites.

The delegation selected by the Clinton administration to represent the United States at the inauguration consisted of many African Americans from all walks of life. On the flight to and from South Africa, Powell had the opportunity to meet Jesse Jackson, the civil rights leader, as well as a host of black political leaders—all of whom were Democrats. They didn't get Powell, this black military man who had served Republican presidents. Several jokingly said to him that he should switch parties and run for president as a Democrat. Powell laughed at the thought, but he welcomed the opportunity to close the gap between himself and other black leaders, so many of whom were suspicious of any African American who was identified as a Republican.

Powell also undertook a more serious mission to Haiti at the request of President Clinton and former President Jimmy Carter. Powell had dealt with the Haitian refugee crisis when he was chairman of the JCS, but now he was being asked to become part of a diplomatic mission sent by the U.S. government to tell the military in Haiti that they had to give up power—or face invasion by American forces. In September 1994, the UN had authorized the use of military force to overthrow the Haitian military and restore the government of the elected president, Jean-Bertrand Aristide, who had been overthrown in a coup. President Clinton announced that U.S. troops would invade Haiti unless Aristide was restored. At this point, Carter proposed sending a high-level delegation to meet with the military government. It was a last-ditch effort to avoid bloodshed.

Powell was not sure if Carter's freelance diplomacy was such a good idea. Nor did Clinton, but the president said to Powell that he would allow the former president to try his hand—for a few days, no longer. If the military in Haiti refused to go, Clinton vowed that he would invade the country. The delegation consisted of Carter, Powell, and Senator Sam Nunn of Georgia. When they arrived in Haiti, Powell was struck by the abject poverty of the country and the contrasting lifestyles of the elites in government and business. Carter, as spokesman for the group, let it be known in no uncertain terms that the military regime had to go. It was their choice—resign or be invaded. Powell was impressed by Carter's firmness and his refusal to give up. He respected the former president's hope to avoid bloodshed and to spare American boys and girls and the poor people of Haiti from the horror of a shooting war. But the military chiefs of Haiti hesitated. In Washington, President Clinton, on the phone with Carter and Powell, said firmly that once time had run out, the soldiers would be sent in. Carter asked for a few more hours and kept on trying. Just as the paratroopers were about to take off from the United States, the Haitian military rulers agreed to give up power. On October 15, 1994, American troops entered Haiti peacefully, and President Aristide was restored to power.

The Haiti mission was one way that Powell's name was kept before the American public. He may have been out of uniform and with no official role, but he was in the minds of his countrymen—and many of them were touting him as a presidential candidate in 1996. All the talk was flattering, but after a while, it became something Powell had to deal with. First, he would have to decide if he wanted to run. It was not easy to put off so many people who wanted him for the highest office in the land. He had always been brought up to believe in service and duty, and if his country called him, could he refuse? Many of the political polls were clear and, for Powell, disturbing: a majority of voters said they would consider casting a ballot for him if he were the nominee.

But running for public office, especially the presidency of the United States, is more than just a personal commitment. It's a commitment for your entire family for the duration of a lengthy campaign that lasts at least two grueling years. And the outcome would be life-changing not only for the nominee but also for his entire family—even if he lost. The family of a president is forever changed by the presidency. All privacy is gone, forever, even after the president leaves the White House. Family members are placed under a relentless spotlight. It is no longer possible for them just to walk the streets, go shopping, or meet a friend for a movie and din-ner. In a way, a president and his family belong to the nation, even after they leave the White House.

And in the preceding 30 years, presidential departures from the White House had not always been pleasant. One president was assassinated (Kennedy), one chose not to run again in the wake of an unpopular war (Johnson), another resigned in disgrace (Nixon), and three were defeated for reelection (Ford, Carter, and Bush).

In the end, Powell realized that anyone who seeks the presidency has to really want it—deep in his gut. That desire was referred to as the "fire in the belly" by some commentators. And Powell gradually came to realize that he did not have that fire. He had served with honor, and he realized he would gladly serve again—but not in an office that required his family to sacrifice so much. After years of separations and moves all over the globe, Powell believed that his family deserved special consideration in this decision.

But the clamor for his candidacy would not go away on its own. By 1995, the media frenzy over Powell's possible run for the presidency was in full force. He could not go anywhere without a microphone being thrust in his face and a reporter asking if he was running for president. After long discussions with Alma, Mike, Linda, and Annemarie, Powell called a press conference for November 8, 1995, at the Ramada Plaza Hotel in Alexandria, Virginia. With his family at his side, Powell told the packed news conference and the American people why he had decided not to seek the presidency, stating that "to offer myself as a candidate for presi-dent requires a commitment and a passion to run the race and to succeed in the quest—the kind of passion and the kind of commitment that I felt every day of my thirty-five years as a soldier, a passion and commitment that, despite my every effort, I do not yet have for political life, because such a life requires a calling that I do not yet hear."[1]

And with that, the torment of the presidential rumors were put to a rest. Powell was still one of the most respected figures in the United States, and the Republican Party claimed him as their own. But now he was free to pursue causes that really interested him. The Colin L. Powell Elementary School in Woodlands, Texas, was a source of special pride and joy. Invitations to join the board of directors of Howard University and the United Negro College Fund gave Powell the opportunity to partici-pate in organizations and institutions dedicated to the improvement of the lives of African Americans. In 1995, Powell's autobiography, *My American Journey*, was published, and like many well-known authors, Powell embarked on a cross-country tour to promote the book and to meet ordinary people at bookstores. For Powell and his family, it was a good time, a time to look in other directions after years in the military.

The Republican Party, however, was not through with one if its favorite public figures. With Powell out of the race, the 1996 Republican presidential nomination was won by former Senator Bob Dole of Kansas. Dole chose Jack Kemp, a former Congressman and Secretary of Housing and Urban Development, as his vice-presidential running mate. Powell was asked to make a prime time address before the Republican National Convention. It was an opportunity for the party to showcase one of the country's most popular figures—but also to show that it was a party of diversity, that there were such people as Republican African Americans.

For Powell, such an address was an excellent opportunity not only to put forth his vision of the future, but also to gently lecture the Republican Party about the need to be more inclusive and not to seem like a party of right-wing, socially conservative white people. In his address before the convention, Powell stated: "The Republican Party must always be the party of inclusion.... It is our diversity that has made us strong."[2] He also made it clear that he supported a woman's right to choose whether or not to have an abortion, and he came out strongly for affirmative action. These two positions were clearly at odds with a majority of the delegates. Powell received only slight applause, and there were a few boos from the delegates. But he was too big a figure in America not to be treated with respect, even if his opinions were in the minority.

So what made him a Republican? On fiscal issues—government expenditures, defense spending, and the like—Powell was a conservative. He did not believe in spending the taxpayers' money on programs of questionable effectiveness and on weapons they did not need. But on social issues—a woman's right to choose, affirmative action, and so on—he was out of step with many other Republicans. That did not matter to him or to Bob Dole, the nominee. They both believed in the "big-tent" theory of American political parties: a political party is big enough to hold many different and even conflicting points of view.

If Powell's endorsement of Dole made him uneasy about his relationship with President Clinton, he didn't show it. Some people criticized Powell for endorsing and campaigning for the opponent of his recent commander in chief. But Powell was self-assured enough to take a political stance for the things he believed in and at the same time to maintain a cordial relationship with Clinton. Clinton, for his part, was always friendly to Powell when they met in public, before and after the election, although he was clearly disappointed that he did not have Powell's support.

In the end, Dole was badly beaten, and Clinton went on to a stormy second term during which he was impeached for lying about a sexual relationship he had had with a White House intern, Monica Lewinsky. During Clinton's travails, Powell kept a low political profile, focusing his energies after 1997 on a new project that he helped start—a nonprofit organization called America's Promise: The Alliance for Youth.

The organization came into being following the Presidents' Summit for America's Future, a meeting sponsored by President Clinton and former presidents Bush, Carter, and Ford, and former first lady Nancy Reagan. The conference was held in Philadelphia from April 27–29, 1997, and its purpose was to challenge the nation to make youth a national priority. Also in attendance were governors, mayors, community leaders, and well-known media personalities from across the country, including the enormously popular and influential Oprah Winfrey. The opening of the meeting was carried live on national and cable television, a sign of the importance the organization's founders attached to its objectives. The summit called for a commitment on the part of the nation to fulfill "Five Promises," which then became the mission statement of America's Promise. They were:

1. Ongoing relationships with caring adults in their lives—parents, mentors, tutors, or coaches;
2. Safe places with structured activities during nonschool hours;
3. Healthy start and future;
4. Marketable skills through effective education; and
5. Opportunities to give back through public service.[3]

As the founding chairman, Powell's reputation and high esteem among the American public were crucial in getting the organization off to a strong start. After several years, America's Promise had more than 500 allied organizations, called "Partners," who agreed to fulfill one or more of the promises by expanding existing youth programs or creating new ones. Among the Partners were corporations, nonprofit organizations, higher-education and faith-based groups, federal agencies, and arts and cultural organizations. By working at the grassroots level, the Partners hope to bring meaningful changes to their communities and to direct young people to a better future.

For Powell, a child of Harlem and the Bronx, America's Promise was close to his heart. He had reminded the Republican Party that there were many people still in need in the country. But equally important, there was the need to do something about it, and the volunteerism and the basis of

America's Promise was directly connected to Powell's personal belief in service and in helping those less fortunate in life.

Powell's refusal to run for president in 1996 basically put to rest speculation about his candidacy in 2000, although there were always voices clamoring for him to seek the presidency. In 2000, Bill Clinton, having served two terms, was not eligible to run for another. The Democratic candidate was likely to be Vice President Al Gore. But the Republican nomination was more competitive. The early favorite was Governor George W. Bush of Texas, the son of former President George Bush. Even before the Republican National Convention, Powell had become an unpaid foreign-policy adviser to Governor Bush, whose international experience was limited. They were not close friends, although Powell had met the younger Bush when his father was president. Because of the high regard that the elder Bush had for Powell, the younger Bush included him in a team of seasoned advisers—many of whom had served President Bush between 1989 and 1993. The advisers included former Defense Secretary Dick Cheney and Condoleezza Rice, a Stanford University professor and a member of the National Security Council in the early 1990s. If George W. Bush was elected, many commentators assumed that his Secretary of State would be Colin Powell. After a spirited challenge by Senator John McCain of Arizona, Bush pulled ahead and was nominated by the Republican Party for President. He selected his father's old friend and colleague Cheney to be his vice presidential running mate.

The office of Secretary of State is the premier cabinet position, and an office of enormous prestige. Powell refused to speculate on his chances to be appointed, but many former colleagues stated publicly that he would be perfect for the job. Former Defense Secretary Caspar Weinberger said that Powell's experience in the military and the executive branches as well as his deliberative style were exactly the traits needed by the nation's chief diplomat.

But the appointment almost never happened. The 2000 election turned out to be one of the closest and most disputed in American history. Bush lost the popular vote to Gore by more than 600,000 votes. But it was electoral votes that mattered, and here, the election hinged on an almost evenly divided vote count in Florida. Whoever won Florida would be the next president. For more than a month, Gore's forces challenged the outcome in court, since Florida state officials had declared Bush the winner by a few hundred votes. Finally, the U.S. Supreme Court ordered the recounting to stop—which left the original decision of the Florida state election board in place: Bush was the winner by 537 votes. George W.

Bush was thus elected president with 271 electoral votes—one more than needed to win.

During the tense wait between election day in November and the Court's decision in December, Powell was seen at Bush's side, usually at his ranch in Crawford, Texas. It was essential that the relatively inexperienced Bush project an image of having seasoned advisers at his side. After the turmoil of the final two Clinton years in office, with the presidency itself tarnished by a sex scandal and the nation bitterly divided by an impeachment trial, there was something reassuring about seeing Colin Powell beside the president-elect. Powell was regarded as a beacon of morality and honesty, a man who told the truth, no matter how difficult the circumstances. And so, almost no one was surprised when George W. Bush nominated Colin Powell to be the 65th Secretary of State of the United States. For Powell, this highest honor soon became a crucible in which he and the nation were tested in ways no one could have imagined.

NOTES

1. Powell, My American Journey, p. 601.

2. Address to the Republican National Convention; excerpts reprinted on the Web at http://robtsheperd.tripod.com/html. July 2002.

3. The Five Promises reprinted from America's Promise Web site, http://www. americaspromise.org. July 2002. Copyright © 2000 America's Promise—The Alliance for Youth.

Chapter 12

SECRETARY OF STATE: PURSUING PEACE IN A VIOLENT WORLD

Colin Powell was sworn in as Secretary of State at the White House on January 20, 2001. He had sailed through his confirmation hearings three days earlier before the U.S. Senate and was approved unanimously. In his prepared remarks before the Senate Foreign Relations committee three days earlier, Powell had said: "We will need to work together well because we have a great challenge before us. But it is not a challenge of survival anymore; it is a challenge of leadership. For it is not a dark and dangerous ideological foe we confront as we did for all those years, but now it is the overwhelming power of millions of people who have tasted freedom. It is our own incredible success, the success of the values that we hold dear, that has given us the challenges that we now face."[1]

Republicans and Democrats alike welcomed Powell's appointment, especially after the turmoil of impeachment and the sour feelings left after President Clinton's acquittal at his Senate trial in January 1999. The State Department eagerly awaited Powell's arrival. The first African American to hold the office of Secretary of State, Powell succeeded the first woman to hold the position—Madeleine Albright, who served from 1997 to 2001 during Clinton's second term. Albright had tangled with Powell when she was UN ambassador and had pushed for U.S. military intervention in the civil war raging in the former Yugoslavia, but in his comments at his confirmation hearing, he praised Albright for her leadership during difficult times. But the general malaise in the last years of Clinton's presidency had lowered morale in the department. Powell was greeted by State Department employees with an almost ecstatic rapture. Now things would get better, many believed, and the department would be restored to its former glory.

Any administration—and especially a new administration—takes time to get adjusted and find its voice. The executive branch of the U.S. government is a vast enterprise employing tens of thousands of people, including career civil service people who stay on from one administration to the next. These people are very important; they are not necessarily the makers of policy, but those who must carry it out, regardless of who is secretary or president.

Powell was only one cabinet member, and cabinet members always have different points of view about policies. President George W. Bush's cabinet was filled with a number of highly experienced and strong personalities. In addition to Powell, Bush had appointed Donald H. Rumsfeld as Secretary of Defense. Rumsfeld had held the job 24 years earlier, from 1975 to 1977, under President Gerald R. Ford. He was known as a brilliant manager with a forceful style that combined strength and wit. He was not at all afraid to fight for what he believed was right and was quite used to getting his way. The same could be said for Vice President Dick Cheney, who had been the Defense Secretary under President George Bush from 1989 to 1993. At 60, Cheney was older than the new president. His presence gave the administration an image of maturity and a link to the successes—namely the Persian Gulf War—of the first President Bush. The other leading foreign policy adviser was Condoleezza Rice, the National Security Adviser, considered brilliant, conservative, and with strong opinions on the major foreign policy and defense issues of the moment. She had been close to Bush on a day-by-day basis during the campaign, and in her new position, she occupied an office in the West Wing of the White House just a few feet away from the president's. She thus could see the president face-to-face at almost any time, which cabinet secretaries, in their headquarters away from the White House, could not do.

In addition to these four figures, there were countless undersecretaries, deputy secretaries, assistant secretaries, and presidential advisers, all of whom contributed to policy debates. In the early months of the administration, a number of hot-button issues emerged and were covered extensively by the media. The president was adamant about building a missile defense system, a shield that would guard against missile attacks from hostile nations. Bush saw the proposed system as purely defensive, but Russia was strongly opposed to it.

Just as with Reagan's space-based SDI program, the Russians and Chinese saw Bush's missile defense as an aggressive posture by the United States designed to weaken them militarily. In addition, America's European allies were uneasy about the missile program. But the administration insisted—loudly and aggressively—that it would pursue a missile defense regardless of what any other country said or did. Rumsfeld and Rice in particular gave public statements to the media, but little was heard from Powell. It is not clear that Powell was necessarily opposed to a missile defense program, but his job required him to deal with the diplomatic fallout. As such, he tended to work behind the scenes and out of the public spotlight.

Another early diplomatic crisis of sorts came about when Bush announced that the United States would no longer support an international environmental agreement negotiated by the Clinton administration. The so-called Kyoto Protocols, named after the city in Japan where the negotiations had taken place, were aimed at reducing global warming by decreasing toxic emissions through a series of agreed-upon goals that the treaty nations would work toward. Although the treaty had not been submitted to the Senate for approval, the Clinton administration announced that as an act of good faith it would voluntarily follow its provisions.

Soon after he became President, Bush announced that the United States would no longer support the Kyoto agreement because, in his view, it would cause serious damage to the American economy. His position was publicly—and strongly—defended by Rice. European allies were angry, and much of the American media blasted the administration, accusing it of following policies on its own that would damage the environment. By going off on its own, regardless of the feelings of its allies, the Bush administration was accused of unilateralism. America's allies wanted to know where Powell was during all this, since he was regarded as one of the world's leading multilateralists—someone who believed in forging a consensus with allies and in seeking common ground on all major issues. What exactly had his advice been on the Kyoto Protocols and on missile defense?

Critics hinted darkly that Powell had been pushed aside by Bush's more conservative advisers, that he really had little or no influence with the president. The questions about Powell's place in the administration were heightened by a controversial statement he made about North Korea. When he stated that the Bush administration would "pick up where the Clinton administration had left off" in negotiating with the North Koreans about their sale of missiles to other countries, the White House quickly corrected his statement. Powell was forced to back down the next day, saying that he had gotten a bit ahead of the president on the issue. It was a terribly embarrassing moment, and it contributed to further rumors that Powell was out of step with the other players in the administration, who were seen as hard-liners and less compromising than the Secretary of State.

It was clear that Powell did not believe the United States should go it alone, doing whatever it felt was necessary even if a policy was at odds with that of its allies. But the characterizations of Cheney, Rumsfeld, and Rice as unilateralists were gross oversimplifications that ignored how government policy is made and the role that individuals play in its formation. For Powell, all the discussions about how much influence he did or did not have within the administration were annoying. He said pointedly to a *Time* magazine reporter that "I've never seen the situation where I haven't been able to work within this Administration. 'Do it my way or else I walk'—it's not my style."[2] And that, of course, was the point that many commentators missed. His style was to work as a loyal member of a team. Powell's experience in the military as well as all his service in government was not about pushing his own personal agenda above all else. As he told *Time*, his job was to give the president his best advice, and in the end, the president made the decision.

As Secretary of State, Powell hoped to strengthen U.S. alliances and to expand NATO. He wanted to strengthen the relationship with China. And, not surprisingly, he wanted to help bring peace to the Middle East and the Persian Gulf.[3] Still, the media persisted in questioning where Powell stood in relation to other advisers. Was he frustrated? Would he resign and thus humiliate the administration? Why was he seemingly so silent while other officials, especially Rice and the media-savvy Rumsfeld, were before the cameras almost on a daily basis? The speculation was at its high point during the summer of 2001.

Then came Tuesday, September 11, 2001.

Even though that date was only seven and one-half months into the Bush administration, it will probably mark the dividing line in the president's term—after September 11, everything changed. On that sunny morning in New York and Washington, terrorists flew hijacked commercial jetliners into the World Trade Center and the Pentagon. A fourth hijacked jet flying toward Washington crashed in a field in western Pennsylvania, its final destination thwarted by passengers who apparently attacked the hijackers before the plane reached the nation's capital. In New York, the two towers of the World Trade Center collapsed in flames killing some 2,800 people. At the Pentagon, 189 died.

As the terrorist attacks unfolded, Colin Powell was in Lima, Peru, preparing to sit down for breakfast with the president of that country, Alejandro Toledo. An aide handed him a note saying that an airplane had crashed into the World Trade Center. Powell said, "Oh my God, a terrible thing has happened"; he prepared to return to Washington immediately. The president had been in Florida that morning visiting an elementary school when word of the attacks reached him. The Secret Service, which is responsible for the president's security, sent him to two air force bases in the South and Midwest before judging that the situation was secure enough for him to return to the White House. At one point on that terrible first night, President and Mrs. Bush were rushed into a bomb shelter of the White House in their nightclothes after air force radar detected what they thought was a plane heading toward the White House on a suicide mission. It was a false alarm. Powell arrived in the nation's capital late that evening and prepared to meet with the president and other cabinet officials the next morning.

Within a matter of days, the American government was able to determine that the attacks had been the work of the worldwide terrorist organization Al-Qaeda, headed by the wealthy Saudi Osama bin-Laden. Bin-Laden's large family was prominent in Saudi Arabia, but they had disavowed him when he adopted the path of terrorism against the United States, claiming to seek revenge for America's desecration of sacred Islamic soil when U.S. forces arrived in Saudi Arabia in 1990. In the years preceding the attacks of September 11, Al-Qaeda had been associated with numerous acts of terrorism against Americans and American targets. They were connected to the bombings of the American embassies in Kenya and Tanzania in 1998 that had killed hundreds of innocent people, most of them Africans. They were also connected with the suicide bombing of a U.S. Navy destroyer, the USS *Cole*, in 1999 when it visited the port city of Aden, Yemen.

There was no question that the United States would respond to the attacks of September 11. Terrorism against the United States meant war, but this would be the first war not against another country with fixed boundaries but against a worldwide secret organization with cells in more than 60 countries. Al-Qaeda clearly had millions of dollars at its disposal, some of it from Arab states that supported terrorist activities. It could afford to train thousands of its adherents all over the world. It had paid for the flying lessons that some of the 19 hijackers took in the years preceding the attacks of September 11. The military war against this new kind of enemy would not be easy to fight. Bin-Laden and his associates had taken refuge in the 1990s in Afghanistan, where a sympathetic government (Islamic fundamentalists called the Taliban) had given him free rein to set up training camps and stockpile weapons. The United States demanded that the government of Afghanistan hand over Osama bin-Laden. When they did not, the United States made plans to overthrow the Taliban regime in Afghanistan and, it was hoped, flush out Al-Qaeda.

That part of the war—which would be called Operation Enduring Freedom—would be the responsibility of the Defense Department and the military services. Powell's State Department would have to fight the diplomatic war: firming up a coalition of nations in the struggle against terrorism, dealing with the difficult balancing act of going after a funda-mentalist Muslim while holding America's Muslim allies in place and not making the conflict seem like an anti-Muslim war; and dealing with an-other conflict that was not directly connected with the war on terrorism but which lurked behind it and threatened America's efforts: the never-ending war between Israel and its Arab neighbors.

Dealing with this network of complicated problems was exactly what Powell was good at. First of all, people thought of him as an honest bro-ker—someone who could be fair to all points of view. The perception of him among America's allies as a moderate in a conservative administra-tion served him well at this time. People also thought of him as a problem solver, a cautious and patient man who would work tirelessly and never give up, even in the face of incredible odds. The military part of the con-flict would get most of the headlines. Powell's work would be behind the scenes, where he patiently constructed alliances, reassured nervous Euro-pean allies, and assured America's Arab friends in the Middle East of U.S. fairness.

In the weeks following the attacks, Powell's job was made easier by the worldwide surge of sympathy for the people of the United States. Amer-ica's traditional allies like Great Britain, Germany, Italy, and other NATO countries immediately pledged their solidarity in the war against terror-ism. But even nations that had been lukewarm toward the United States—and even hostile to it (Cuba, for example)—expressed their sup-port for the United States and their revulsion to terrorism. Most countries realized that weapons of terror could be used against any country, whether a democracy or a dictatorship.

The European allies needed no persuasion to support the U.S. fight against terrorism, but they did want Powell to assure them that the United States would also do all it could to resolve the Israeli-Palestinian conflict. To this end, Powell called European allies on a regular basis to re-port on his telephone conversations with Israeli Prime Minister Ariel Sharon and Palestinian leader Yasser Arafat. He made similar calls to of-ficials in the Saudi government, where he still had contacts going back to the Persian Gulf War in 1991. Another important figure Powell kept in touch with was President Vladimir Putin of Russia. Putin enjoyed a good relationship with President Bush, and Powell's concern that the Russian leader be kept informed helped keep that country in line with American policy in the war against terror.

On October 7, 2001, Operation Enduring Freedom began with a fero-cious air assault on Taliban and Al-Qaeda positions in Afghanistan.

Eventually, as many as 7,000 U.S. troops entered the country along with forces from other allied nations such as Great Britain and Canada. The Taliban were defeated in a matter of weeks, although pockets of Al-Qaeda and pro-Taliban forces continued to attack allied positions and attempted to destabilize the new government established in Kabul, the Afghan capital.

A more difficult problem for Powell was Pakistan, where anti-American fervor threatened the government of President Pervez Musharraf, who was cooperating with the United States. Many Al-Qaeda forces fled into Pakistan, whose border areas with Afghanistan were mountainous and under the control of local ethnic groups who ignored the Pakistani government in Islamabad. In order to bolster the Musharraf government, Bush and Powell pushed for a removal of long-standing U.S. sanctions against the Pakistanis for their building of nuclear weapons. Pakistan was now an ally by necessity, and previous policies needed to be reconsidered in the interests of the greater war on terrorism. Powell's hair-raising flight into Islamabad in the fall of 2001 (see chapter 1) was one part of his mission to make sure that the government of Pakistan remained loyal to the war on terrorism, despite the powerful anti-American sentiment among many groups in the country.

When Pakistan came close to war with its neighbor India in late 2001 and early 2002, Powell's diplomatic efforts were complicated. If war broke out between Pakistan and India, Pakistani troops would be pulled from the western border with Afghanistan and redeployed eastward, to the Indian border. Such a development would be a blow to the efforts to track and capture Al-Qaeda forces that had fled Afghanistan and were hiding in western Pakistan. Powell made daily calls to the leaders of India and Pakistan imploring them to hold off on war. By early 2003 tensions remained high, but war had not broken out.

Other countries around the world with large Muslim populations also presented unique diplomatic challenges to Powell. Indonesia, in southeast Asia, which had the largest Muslim population of any country, was a hotbed of anti-Americanism among the population. Not much could be done diplomatically except to shore up the government, which was not anti-American but had to deal with anti-American feelings among its people. Nearby, in the Philippines, a violent Muslim minority demanding independence was causing havoc in parts of the country, including kidnapping and murdering American civilians, some of them Christian missionaries. The Philippines, a former American colony, had a long relationship with the United States that included their liberation from Japanese occupation by American forces in 1944 and 1945. The Philippine constitution prohibited foreign troops from fighting on Philippine soil, so all the Americans could do to help the government fight the Muslim insurrection was to send advisers to teach the Philippine army how to fight an insurgency.

Then there was the question of Israel and the Palestinians. The Bush administration fervently tried to ignore the connection between its war on terrorism and its support of Israel, but the reality was that much of the anti-Americanism found in the Muslim world could be traced to America's unstinting support—financial, military, and moral—for Israel. Even though the United States pumped billions of dollars in aid to Arab countries, including Egypt and the Palestinian authority, Arabs especially felt the United States was biased toward Israel at the expense of the oppressed Palestinian people. This festering belief poisoned the efforts to attack terrorism that originated from the Muslim world, especially that part of it in the Middle East. (Most of the hijackers on September 11 were Saudi nationals by birth.)

Bush was reluctant to get involved with the Israeli-Palestinian issue because, in his opinion, the Clinton administration had gone too far in trying to broker a deal. When the deal fell through, violence erupted. Powell's specific views at this early period in the administration are not known, but as someone who advocated caution before involvement, it is probably safe to say that he did not disagree with the president. Better, he felt, to let the two sides work out their own problems, at least until American involvement could make a significant contribution toward ending the conflict.

But this stance proved more and more difficult to hold. By the spring of 2002, the violence between Israel and the Palestinians had worsened, in particular, one disturbing development that threatened to plunge the region into chaos. That development was the increase in the number of Palestinian suicide bombings against Israeli civilians. Some Palestinian men and women strapped dynamite to their bodies and mixed with Israeli civilians—on crowded streets, at bus stops, on buses, in discos or restaurants—then detonated the explosives, killing themselves and their Israeli victims. After a number of deadly suicide bombings, Prime Minister Sharon ordered the Israeli army into Palestinian-controlled areas of the West Bank. The Arab world was irate, accusing the Israelis aggression against the Palestinians. The Israelis, in turn, called the suicide bombers terrorists, not oppressed Palestinians, and blamed Yasser Arafat for the killings.

Powell took a middle road after the first Israeli incursion. He had always spoken out forcefully against the suicide bombings, calling on Arafat to rein in the terrorists. Now he also urged restraint on the part of the Israelis, calling on them to pull back their forces as soon as possible. Most of the Arab media saw Powell's call to the Israelis as weak and ineffective. They complained that "as soon as possible" was not as strong as "immediately." But both Bush and Powell were in a difficult position. They believed that the Israelis, just like the Americans, had a right to defend themselves in the face of terrorist attacks.

By April 2002, Bush and Powell felt it necessary to change course. The president realized the United States could no longer stand by as the suicide bombings continued and as the Arab world boiled with rage against Israel and the United States. Something had to be done, if for no other reason than the fact that the Israeli-Palestinian conflict was threatening the war against terrorism. It was time for Colin Powell to go to the Middle East and meet with both sides. Meeting with Arafat, however, presented a problem. The Israeli army had entered the West Bank city of Ramallah, where Arafat had his headquarters, and had surrounded his house with tanks. He was basically under house arrest, and no one could enter or leave his compound unless the Israelis approved. For his part, before any meeting, Powell wanted Arafat to denounce terrorism to his people in Arabic (not just to English-speaking journalists). Arafat made a denunciation of terrorism enough to satisfy Powell. The Israelis, however, were not happy that Powell wanted to see Arafat, but in the end, they allowed the Secretary of State to go to Ramallah and meet with the Palestinian leader.

Powell moved back and forth between the Israeli and Palestinian sides. Israeli forces escorted his limousine to the entrance to Arafat's building, where the meeting was held. When the meetings were over, Powell returned to his car, which was then picked up by Israeli army vehicles and escorted back to Jerusalem. After more than a week of meetings, Powell returned to the United States without having achieved a definitive agreement. The Israelis had not withdrawn, and the suicide bombings, although reduced in frequency, continued. Arafat claimed that he could not control terrorism if he was under house arrest; the Israelis refused to negotiate with Arafat because of the terrorism, which they insisted he had unleashed and could control.

Much of the U.S. media returned to the theme that Powell's mission was a failure and he was (again) the odd man out. The media analysis of the situation was speculation. No one knows what advice Powell gave Bush or how much he disagreed (if he did) with the advice of Cheney and Rumsfeld. Several weeks after Powell returned from his trip, the Israelis withdrew their forces from Palestinian territories. But then the suicide bombings began again, and by June, the Israeli army had reentered the areas recently evacuated. As the bloodshed continued, the United States made a crucial decision. Bush announced that it was time for new Palestinian leadership— Arafat had to go. The Israelis were ecstatic. The Arab world was shocked and dismayed. Where would all this lead in terms of the war on terrorism? And what role had Powell played, if any, in this change of policy?

The answer to the latter question was not easy to discover. As always, Powell was the consummate team player. When President Bush announced the change in attitude toward Arafat on June 24, 2002, Powell was at his side. In an interview that day, Powell told a reporter that he had warned Arafat that he had to change if he wanted the United States as a peace partner.[4] Sources within the State Department confirmed that Powell and the department at first were reluctant to abandon Arafat, and that Cheney and Rumsfeld had always argued the hard-line position. But gradually, through long discussions of the options, Powell had come to the conclusion that a change in Palestinian leadership was essential if peace were ever to come to the Middle East. It was time for this change, and he supported the president.

By the middle of 2002, the media were still casting Powell as the moderate in a conservative administration, as the one always arguing for the cautious approach against a group of tough conservatives who always favored a noncompromising approach. The truth? There was no way of knowing precisely who advocated what or when. By the middle of 2002, Powell remained as Secretary of State, a team player and still, in many ways, the star of the cabinet.

But by the middle of 2002, the Bush administration began to focus on another issue in the Middle East: the danger posed by Saddam Hussein's regime in Iraq. The background of the Iraq issue was rooted in the 1991 Persian Gulf War. Despite his army's defeat in that conflict, Saddam Hussein remained in power. In addition, he defied UN resolutions to prove he had gotten rid of his weapons of mass destruction—especially biological and chemical weapons—and in so doing kept his country under UN sanctions, which meant great deprivation and hardship for the average Iraqi.

Some officials in the administration—particularly in the Department of Defense—believed that Iraq was tied in some way to the attacks of September 11. They urged Bush to carry the war against terror to all corners of the globe, especially Iraq, which presented a clear target with a history of aggression against its neighbors and a dictator who was universally reviled.

But the administration did not present the case against Iraq to the public in such broad terms. Instead, it focused on what it insisted were Iraq's possession of weapons of mass destruction and the threat they presented to the world. Some voices in the administration argued that peace would never come to the Middle East as long as Saddam Hussein remained in power and that the United States needed to make a preemptive strike—on its own, if necessary—to remove the dictator. Others, however, believed that before war, broad support from the international community was essential for American credibility. That support would have to come only through the backing of the United Nations.

Powell convinced President Bush to address the United Nations to lay out the case against Iraq and to insist that the international organization finally do something more than issue resolutions that were routinely ignored by Saddam Hussein. Bush spoke before the General Assembly on September 12, 2002, a year and one day after the terrorist attacks on the United States, and his speech was well-received. After the speech, Powell's job was to work behind the scenes at the UN to craft a forceful resolution that would have the backing of the Security Council—no easy task, since some of America's leading European allies (France and Germany, in particular) were very uneasy about using force or even threatening force against Iraq.

But Powell's brilliance as a diplomat shined in these critical weeks. Much to the astonishment of the world, he was able to get a resolution that passed unanimously on November 12, 2002. It called on Iraq to admit UN weapons inspectors into the country to search for weapons of mass destruction and to eliminate any that were found. At the end of the resolution—known as Resolution 1441—was a critical sentence. It stated that "the council has repeatedly warned Iraq that it will face serious consequences as a result of its continued violations of its obligations."[5] The term "serious consequences" would become an object of great debate in the months ahead.

After vacillating and employing delaying tactics, the Iraqis finally allowed the UN weapons inspectors into the country by the end of 2002. Their work was slow and laborious, and as the weeks passed, it was clear that the United States and its main ally, Great Britain, were growing increasingly frustrated by the inspection process and by what it claimed was Iraq's trickery and deceit. Germany, France, and Russia insisted that the process be given more time. However, when they announced that they would oppose all use of force against Iraq—and would work within the United Nations to defeat any U.S.-sponsored resolution authorizing force—Powell believed that these countries had crossed the line. From this point on, in early 2003, Powell became an ardent and strong proponent for the use of force against Iraq. For some observers, it seemed a shift in position from the Powell of late 2002, who had worked the diplomatic channels to get a unanimous resolution with teeth in it confronting the Iraqis. Now, however, he felt betrayed by three principal U.S. allies. The French, Germans, and Russians had every right to oppose the policy, but to work actively to defeat and humiliate the United States at the UN was unprecedented and unacceptable.

Powell appeared again before the UN and demanded that it put steel in its backbone and not allow the Iraqis to get away with their deceits again. The French, Germans, and Russians, however, would not budge. A new resolution faced defeat in the Security Council. Therefore, the United States and Great Britain decided simply that they did not need one, that Resolution 1441, with its threat of "serious consequences" was, in fact, sufficient for the use of military force.

On March 26, 2003, the United States and Great Britain invaded Iraq from the neighboring country of Kuwait. After what seemed to be a faltering start, U.S. and British forces defeated the Iraqi army in about a month. Saddam Hussein disappeared—no one was sure if he had died in one of the massive air attacks or had simply gone underground hoping to retrieve power on another day—and the United States settled in for what promised to be a troubled period of occupation during which American forces were attacked on a daily basis. In addition, the weapons of mass destruction had not been found by the summer of 2003, leading to harsh critiques of American and British intelligence and to growing doubts about the reasons presented to the public for going to war.

With Iraq still brewing, Powell almost immediately turned his attention to the Israeli-Palestinian issue. In 2002, the Bush administration put forth a plan—called "the Roadmap"—that outlined the steps and a timetable under which Israel would withdraw from most of the occupied territories it had held since the 1967 war, and an independent state of Palestine would be established. In return, the Palestinians would renounce all violence against Israel, including suicide bombings against civilians.

Powell crisscrossed the globe tirelessly in search of peace not only in the Middle East but in Asia and other parts of the world. At 66, he was in good physical shape although no longer a young man. Speculation that he would retire at the end of President Bush's first term in 2005 drew a denial from Powell, but many observers believed that Alma and his family would definitely prefer that he return to private life after four years at State. Powell's responsibilities were perhaps greater than any Secretary of State in the post–World War II era. Yet he seemed to bear his burdens with the same grace, calmness, and self-assuredness that he possessed throughout his career in the military and the civilian government.

NOTES

1. U.S. Department of State, *Confirmation hearings by Colin L. Powell*, 17 January 2001. Full text at http://www.state.gov.

2. Johanna McGeary, "Odd Man Out," *Time*, 10 September 2001, p. 32.

3. Ibid., pp. 30–31.

4. Todd S. Purdum, "Powell Says He Warned Arafat to Shift Course or Be Left Behind," *New York Times*, 25 June 2002.

5. The full text of Security Council Resolution 1441 may be found at the United Nations Web site, http://www.un.org.

BIBLIOGRAPHY

For up-to-the minute information on Secretary of State Powell's policy positions, statements, and schedule, see the State Department's Web site, http://www.state.gov. This site is also an excellent resource for information about the Department and its role in American history.

For information on America's Promise: The Alliance for Youth, the organization Colin Powell cofounded, see http://www.americaspromise.org.

BOOKS AND ARTICLES

Duffy, Michael. "Better Late Than Never." *Time*, 15 April 2002.

Gordon, Michael R., and Bernard E. Trainor. *The Generals' War: The Inside Story of the Conflict in the Gulf*. Boston: Little, Brown, 1996.

Halberstam, David. *War in a Time of Peace: Bush, Clinton, and the Generals*. New York: Scribner, 2001.

Harari, Oren. "Behind Open Doors: Powell's Seven Laws of Leadership." *Modern Maturity*, February 2002.

———. *"The Leadership Secrets of Colin Powell*. New York: McGraw-Hill, 2002.

Keller, Bill. "The World According to Powell." *New York Times Magazine*, 25 November 2001.

McGeary, Johanna. "Odd Man Out." *Time*, 10 September 2001.

Pelley, Scott. Interview with Colin Powell broadcast on CBS, 3 April 2002. Text of interview available CBS Web site: http://www.state.gov.

Powell, Colin L., with Joseph E. Persico. *My American Journey*. New York: Ballantine, 1995.

Purdum, Todd. S. "Powell Says He Warned Arafat to Shift Course or Be Left Be-
    hind." *New York Times*, 25 June 2002.
Rosenberg, Matthew J. "Son of Jamaican Immigrants Becomes Secretary of
    State." *Associated Press*, January, 2001.
Sipress, Alan. "Policy Divide Thwarts Powell." *Washington Post*, 26 April 2002.
Steins, Richard. *The Mideast After the Gulf War.* Brookfield, Conn.: Millbrook,
    1992.
U.S. Department of State. *Confirmation Hearing by Colin Powell.* 17 January 2001.
    Text available at State Department Web site: http://www.state.gov.

INDEX

About the Author

RICHARD STEINS is an editor and author. He has written numerous books and articles on a wide array of subjects.